A BENGALI LADY IN ENGLAND

A Bengali Lady in England

Annotated translation with a critical introduction to
Krishnabhabini Das' *Englandey Bangamahila*

NABANITA SENGUPTA

SHAMBHABI
CALCUTTA | NEW DELHI

SHAMBHABI THE THIRD EYE IMPRINT

33/1/2 K B Sarani, Mall Road, Calcutta 80
70-B/9 Amritpuri, East of Kailash, New Delhi 65

Email thethirdeyeimprint@gmail.com
Website www.hawakal.com

First edition October, 2020

ISBN: 9788194421207
Price: 500 INR | USD 17.99

ACKNOWLEDGEMENTS

This project had begun as a doctoral dissertation submitted in 2015 which is now being published as a book in a slightly reworked form. As I proceeded with my research I realised that this thesis could not have been completed without the unfailing support of many and I owe my sincerest gratitude towards all of them. I am deeply grateful and indebted to Prof. Jharna Sanyal, my supervisor, who has always been an extraordinary source of guidance, encouragement and support. Her patience and faith in this research project have helped me take it towards completion. Her detailed appraisal of my work at every stage and her valuable inputs have not only improved the quality of this work but has also helped me mature as a researcher.

I express my gratitude to all the teachers of the Department of English, University of Calcutta for their insightful suggestions at various stages of my work. Prof Sanjukta Dasgupta has been another pillar of support encouraging me to publish this dissertation in the form of a book.

I am also extremely indebted to my colleagues at Sarsuna College, especially Dr. Sarottama Majumdar and ex Teacher-in-charge Sri Arun Kumar Dawn for easing my college work load and enable me to complete this dissertation. Their encouragement and support has helped me maintain a balance between my job and my research.

The entire staff of the National Library and particularly Sri Asim Mukhopadhyay deserves special thanks for aiding me with my research process. I am also grateful to the staff of the Central Library of the University of Calcutta, Bangiya Sahitya Parishad Library, Chaitanya Library, The Asiatic Society Library, and the Ramkrishna Mission Institute of Culture Library for their kind cooperation during this entire period.

Friends who deserve a special mention are Suranjana Choudhury and Amit Shankar Saha without whose inputs the dissertation could not have been turned to book. Amit has played a key role in introducing me to Kiriti Sengupta and Bitan Chakraborty of *Shambhabi* and *Hawakal* house to whom I express my gratitude for bringing out this book

Lastly and most importantly, I am grateful to my entire family for being there and encouraging me throughout. Without their unfailing support, it would have been impossible to complete this task.

CONTENTS

FIRST PUBLISHER'S NOTE

Author of this book is presently in England with her husband. It is according to her wishes that I have published her manuscript just as it was. Apart from correcting a word here or there, I have not interfered. A work becomes flawless and improves qualitatively if the author can read the proof herself. But circumstances did not permit this here. The author, being in England, could not check the proof at all. Therefore while publishing, the quality of this book has not improved, instead it might have worsened. I hope she will be in India to oversee the printing of the second edition of her book. The language of this text is very simple, lucid and melodious. According to me such an unassuming and composed language is best for writing a book.

Though whatever she has written in this book is not entirely accurate, there is no doubt regarding her noble and virtuous intention. Years of bondage has turned India, the land of our dharma and karma, into a lifeless mass. Mother India is herself *Annapurna*, the provider of food; yet her sons are deprived of it. All of us must have realized this; but to what avail! Years of colonization have turned our bones into dust. To sow the seeds of life here once again the seeds must be brought from the land of spectacular achievements of a zealous race. And there is no doubt that England is that very place. India will need to obtain her ambrosial seeds from England only, especially with the kind of strong ties that has been destined to form between the two countries. Probably this is what the author's motive is. But there is a grave danger in the task of bringing that medication from England; lest an Indian ends up losing his priceless Indian heart by mistaking the poison to be the remedy. This fear is not totally unfounded. I have seen that it is very difficult to resist the temptations of material life. Only the saint who knows how to separate *amrit* from poison can follow the free British race and pull this country out from her present state of degradation.

The author has very clearly talked about this here. We have been greatly benefitted by this young author. She has meticulously explained both the internal and external aspects of a free race and has upheld for us each and every example that constitutes its freedom. The whole of this book is very useful and the final chapters in particular are invaluable. Every reader will have to vociferously acknowledge that her text *Englandey Bangamahila* is an illustration of rich philosophy, hard work and an unadulterated love for one's countrymen.

INTRODUCTION

Women have been confined to the domestic space by tradition and its system of beliefs. Travelling was a taboo for them in most cultures even till recent past. In the nineteenth century, there was a significant rise in the number of women travellers. Most of these women travelled as companions to their husbands or with some close male kin as their chaperone. In India too, in spite of religious orthodoxy and social inhibitions, women started travelling abroad. There were a considerable number of women travellers even from Bengal. The Dutt sisters, Toru and Aru, travelled to Europe with their family (France and England) in 1869, Shashipada Banerjee's wife Rajkumari went to England in 1871. Jnanadanandini Devi (1877)[i] accompanied by her three children, became the first Bengali woman to travel to England without an adult male companion. The list is quite long, but very few women from Bengal kept records of their travels. This void was first filled by a Bengali Hindu housewife belonging to an orthodox family. In 1880, Krishnabhabini Das travelled to England with her husband and in 1885 she brought out her travel narrative on England, *Englandey Bangamahila (A Bengali Lady in England)*, published anonymously from Calcutta. She became the first Bengali woman to write from England though by then, there was an already existing corpus of such travel writings by Bengali men.

Krishnabhabini was born in 1864, to a Brahmin couple in Kajala village. At the age of ten, she was married off to Devendranath Das, the youngest son of Srinath Das. Though she had received elementary education in her childhood, it was Devendranath who took an active interest in her education and personally tutored her[ii]. Due to the limited scope of education available to women of the nineteenth century, quite a number of educated men had taken up the responsibility of educating their wives. Devendranath was one of them. The depth and extent of Krishnabhabini's education is clearly reflected in *Englandey Bangamahila*. Her account is one of the most comprehensive narratives on British race and culture even when compared to other more illustrious travel writers like Romesh Chandra Dutt, Rabindranath Tagore, Keshub Chandra Sen, and others. Written by a woman from the colonies who had no formal education, *Englandey Bangamahila* is remarkable in terms of ethnographic details and comparative study of Bengali and British cultures.

In order to understand *Englandey Bangamahila* in its proper context, it is important to situate it within the tropes of rising nationalism and women's travel writing of the nineteenth century. Along with the rise of Brahmo Samaj and beginning of English education among the middle classes, there was a steep rise in the number of travellers from India. This caused a sudden boom in Indian travel writings as these travellers shared their experiences with fellow countrymen. These counter-narratives critically scrutinised the colonisers' culture and lifestyle. As Codell says, "They wanted to see

Britain and Europe firsthand, judge what their colonizers told them, discover what colonizers did not say, and transmit information to other Indians" (175). These "guest discourses"[iii], became a part of the nineteenth century nation building agenda. The 'gaze' upon the white man brought out the shortcomings of the Europeans and demolished their myth of a superior Eurocentric worldview.

These narratives also focussed on the diversities of European countries and challenged the concept of a homogenous West by comparing various western countries such as England, France, Germany, etc. in their travel writings[iv]. In this way these travel writers made immense contribution towards the building of a national or indigenous identity, as opposed to the identity of the colonizers. Krishnabhabini Das, by recording her experiences in England and making them publicly available, treads upon a similar path. But unlike her contemporary male travellers, this road is both difficult and unique for her as she becomes the first Bengali woman to write about her experiences in England.

As Krishnabhabini mentions in her book, *Englandey Bangamahila* is a result of her nationalist concerns. In fact, the nationalist sentiments are so strongly voiced in this book that the British considered this book dangerous and it was banned in this country (Deb 139). Hence, it is travel writing with a very clear agenda. But it is also the only documentation of her years in England, and can be read as a kind of life writing or autobiographical writing. Unlike the traditional autobiographies, the central focus of the narrative in this text is not upon the authorial 'I'. The 'self' here metamorphoses into a body of thoughts and the personal entity is subsumed within the larger social consciousness. Nevertheless, it involves a particular kind of self-fashioning where the author is analysed not by her actions but by the ideologies and issues that she considers in the text.

Throughout the text there is no mention of the author's personal life in England[v]. The social consciousness of the author as expressed through writing dominates her personal 'self' and the only authorial intervention that we get is through her interpretation and comparison of the two cultures. Her principal concern in the text is the condition of Bengali women back in the country and how that could be improved. Marjanne E. Goose says, "Women's narratives become inseparable from their relationship to others" (415) and this is amply illustrated by Krishnabhabini's awareness and solidarity with the women of her nation.

Englandey Bangamahila is an important text that highlights the socio-cultural history of that period and conforms to the dominant ideologies of the nineteenth century. But beyond all these, there is a distinctive woman's voice, sympathetic to her fellow sufferers. In fact, her concern about other Bengali women, trapped in the traditional Bengali society is the driving force behind this text. Krishnabhabini Das' overwhelming concern about the fate of the Bengali women visible in the issues she chose to represent in her text makes her narrative one about the subjugated women of Bengal. The persona of Krishnabhabini is built up through the way she perceives the existence of her fellow sisters as opposed to the relatively free women of England.

The author becomes inseparable from other women of India who faced the doubly bonded life at every moment of their existence. It reminds us of Rowbotham's concept of 'collective consciousness' that goes into the making of a woman's self, as discussed in Susan Friedman's essay, "Women's autobiographical selves: Theory and Practice". It is this collective consciousness which constitutes Krishnabhabini's psyche and identity.

In Friedman's words it is actually a "sense of shared identity with other women, an aspect of identity that exists in tension with a sense of [her] own uniqueness" (44). It is this tension between the individual identity and the shared identity which adds to the complexities of women's life writings. The individual identity of Krishnabhabini as a woman enjoying relatively greater freedom compared to her fellow sisters contradicts the identity that she gains in solidarity with them. These issues together make Krishnabhabini's work more complex than a mere travelogue.

Nationalism and travel writing being two important concerns of the nineteenth century *Englandey Bangamahila* has often been examined under these lenses. As pointed out by Simonti Sen, "Krishnabhabini clearly resided with her co-travellers in the space constitutive of the nation. Her travel account is cast in the usual frame that separates the 'backward East from the 'progressive West' and engages with all the stock-in-trade nationalist questions" (Travels to Europe 23). But what has been ignored under the impact of these more dominant concerns is the effort that underlies the making of this travel narrative. It is more than evident that for a lady with her background and situation it was not possible to have access to all the places and details she describes in the text. She must have had recourse to other texts on England. The question is how did she use them? Does her use of such text add a special dimension to her narrative?

In the preface to *Englandey Bangamahila* (Bengali Lady in England) Krishnabhabini writes, "To reduce the chances of making mistakes, I have read a few books by some British as well as some foreign authors regarding how the British judge themselves and how the people of other nations look at them. Among those, one particular book on England, written by the great French scholar Taine, has proved to be very useful" (34–35). The book that she refers to is the *Notes on England* by Hyppolite Taine in which the renowned French scholar records his experience of England, a country that he has visited several times for academic and other purposes. Krishnabhabini, a female colonial subject and a newcomer to England uses Taine's text as her source text of information. Before reaching English shores, she had already prepared her frame of mind and her gaze to undertake the task of writing a nationalist text.

Unlike most of the nineteenth century women who were both physically and mentally trapped within the four walls of their houses, Krishnabhabini had a keen awareness of her surrounding and an informed solidarity with the women of her country even when she was in Calcutta. In the poems that she wrote before going abroad, later collected by her in an anthology called *Jeeboner Drishyamala* (Glimpses of my Life), she keeps referring to the difficult and bonded lives of the women of her country. In poems such as *Nanad bondhur proti* (To my sister-in-law, my friend) or *Pakhir Proti* (To a Bird) she laments about the lack of freedom in the lives of Bengali women. She even wrote an entire poem on women's education *Streeshikkhar durobostha darshane* (On seeing the deplorable condition of Women's education) before she left for English shores. Another poem, *Durgotsav o Mandraje Durbhikkho* (Durga puja and Famine in Madras) shows how her concern and empathy goes beyond the boundaries of Bengal and acquires a pan-Indian consciousness.

Taine's detailed analysis of British culture gives her that required base from which she could begin her required exploration. Taine too is an outsider like her but there is a vast difference in their degrees of cultural alienation from England. This difference is reflected throughout *Englandey Bangamahila* through her assimilation, interpretation and rejection of *Notes on England*. These selections are completely hers, determined by her understanding and her consciousness of her times which were formed before she reaches England. That is where the singularity of her text lies.

Taine's Notes on England:

Hilda Laura Norma writes in 1921 that "...the books which throw the most light on (Taine's) shadowy personality are his notes on travel in England and France, his Journey in the Pyrenees, and the few chapters of his unfinished novel Etienne Mayran"(529). In 1872 Hippolyte Taine, the great French scholar and traveller to England published his *Notes sur l'Angleterre* as a column in the Temps in Paris and almost contemporaneously its translation, *Notes on England* was being published in England in The Daily News. Later, W. F. Rae once again translated this book from the French original and published it in 1885, the same year in which *Englandey Bangamahila* was published. Krishnabhabini was probably familiar with the columns of the *Notes* published in The Daily News[vi].

Like Krishnabhabini, Taine's account of England is also not an unequivocal praise of the English race and culture. He was rather "amused by the idiosyncrasies of the English" (Peyre, 276). As Peyre said, "the chief severity of Taine is exercised against the lack of conversation of Englishmen, the prevalence of drunkenness among many of them, rich and poor ... against the fashions in women's clothes... and the hideousness of art..." (276). Such criticisms of the English race highlight the superiority that Taine feels as a French man. But this 'belated racial theorist of French romanticism', Taine continues the legacy of white supremacy by believing in 'the thesis that every genius is determined by two factors – the racial factor and the milieu' (White, 83). Therefore, the English might not appear to him to be as cultured as the French are but while comparing the English with the colonized races, the former definitely appears superior. This approach is starkly in contrast with Krishnabhabini Das' perspectives of race and individual. In fact, though Krishnabhabini draws extensively from Taine's Notes, both of them look at the English race from two ends of the spectrum.

Taine's account of England is an accumulation of his experiences over the years. As Rae says in the introduction to his translation of Taine's *Notes on England,* "In 1861, and subsequently, he visited England with a view of reading in the British Museum, and of seeing the country and people face to face. The *Notes* contained in this volume comprise the frequent observations of ten years. They were all revised after his last visit in 1871" (xxvii). So, Taine's *Notes* is a compilation of his knowledge about England gathered over a decade and revised and re-revised with time, experience and close observation of English culture. His erudition and interest also included English literature and he compiled an extensive History of English Literature which points at his overall familiarity with England and the English. All these together make Taine a dependable source for Krishnabhabini, a female colonial subject with an extremely limited resource.

Krishnabhabini's Taine

There are two kinds of readings that Krishnabhabini engages to understand England. One is the society that she 'reads' through her everyday interaction and the other is her reading at British Library where she comes across Taine's Notes. Some of the passages in Krishnabhabini's work are a direct translation from Taine's Notes which might give the readers a feeling that this book is a Bengali adaptation of Taine's. But a closer analysis dispels every doubt regarding the originality of her text. There are numerous examples where their use of similar information leads to completely different inferences regarding the characteristic traits of the British. In the passages where she directly translates Taine are primarily enumerative and empirical in nature but continues to differ starkly at places which involve a cultural comparison. She too, like Taine is constantly comparing every aspect of British culture with that of her own; what makes the text so interesting is that it shows the way in which Krishnabhabini, a doubly marginalized individual, reads and interprets the culture and lifestyle of her rulers. This deflates the notion of European superiority and their racial pride. Her interpretation also deals a blow to the concept of homogeneity of the white Europeans. By using Taine and yet reaching a different interpretation, she also makes a statement on French culture which she perceives to be different from the English one, though both these European countries share a similar colonial past. Thus a concept of Europe comes out of the reading of these two texts.

In her book, Krishnabhabini questions the very basis of British authority in India by calling them exploiters and oppressors. She goes on to provide a detailed account of the British social structure, lifestyle, politics, culture and economics. Most of the empirical details such as the length of the Suez canal and the cost of building it, details of British Library and other monuments and many more, were largely taken from Taine's Notes on England. Readers can find extensive passages from Taine's work translated and assimilated into Krishnabhabini's travel writing and it becomes a primary text for her—a text which provides her with enumerative details along with an outsider's perspective to England. Taine with his non-British European background would have the objective distance that a travel narrative requires along with an understanding of a culture that was completely alien to her; to such an end she claims to have read both British and non-British authors on England, to understand "how the British judge themselves and how the people of other nations look at them" (34). Taine's work on England has helped her in more than one way. She makes up for her lack of firsthand exposure and experience of the British culture and people by reading up books and journals on these subjects in the British Library. Taine's detailed account provides her with a readymade source material. The new text is a completely different one in its intent, purpose and voice. In spite of modelling her work on Taine's, she remains a voice from the colonies, speaking out against the atrocities of the colonisers as well as highlighting their qualities that make them the greatest power in the nineteenth century. Her voice is scathingly honest while pointing out the flaws in both the cultures and she is successful in creating the text that she is set out to—a text that would help in the nineteenth century nation-building agenda, a self-imposed task of the educated middle class Bengalis.

A few examples of passages from *Englandey Bangamahila* where we find a direct influence of Taine's *Notes on England* are tabulated below. Those in the list are just indicative and randomly selected, in actuality there are many more such passages where Krishnabhabini directly uses the information provided by Taine. They elucidate the ways in which Taine's documentation of England was used by this Bengali woman.

Englandey Bangamahila	*Notes on England*
London is a vast city; the biggest in the world. It is about ten miles in length and eight miles in width. London is about four times bigger and eight times more populated than Calcutta. Forty lakh people reside here. One needs to drive continuously for four to five days to take a complete tour of the city but still, one will not be familiar with all its roads. Though London is already a vast city, it is still expanding (88).	The population numbers three millions and a quarter; that makes twelve cities like Marseilles, ten cities like Lyons, two cities like Paris put together; but words upon paper are no substitutes for the sensation of the eyes. It is necessary to take a cab several days in succession, and proceed straight towards the south, the north, the east, and the west, during a whole morning, as far as the uncertain limits where houses grow scanty and country begins (15).
According to the records in a year about forty thousand ships visit these docks and at a time there are about five to six thousand of them plying on the river Thames or docked in London. It sends shivers down the spines to even think of the amount of wealth these ships extort from other countries (265–66).	A merchant who is the superintending the arrival of spices from Java, and the transshipment of ice from Norway, tells me that about 40, 000 vessels enter every year, and that on an average, there are from 5,000 to 6,000 in the docks or the river at one time (31).
In the country sides, the parsons visit the houses of their parishioners. They affectionately	When I walk to the village with the clergyman, he enters the houses,

enquire after the education of the children and chastise them in case of any wrong doings. They preach against consumption of alcohol, talk to the people about their jobs and advice them on various issues (228).	pats the little ones on the head, gets information about their progress, admonishes the bad boys, speaks against drunkenness, chats with the people about their concerns; he is their natural counsellor (195).

Taine, the French thinker, historian, literary and art critic, visits England as an invited dignitary to Oxford while Krishnabhabini, a Bengali Hindu middleclass woman goes there as a doubly marginalized subject, a housewife from the colonies. So one is European, white, male with the best education and scholarship and another is from the colonies, brown and female, without any kind of formal education. Yet, Krishnabhabini is not awed by this illustrious scholar. Her interpretation of the British society is not influenced by Taine's or anyone else's representation of the same. Her intelligent and perceptive mind can look beyond the colonial politics and understand for herself what lies in the heart of the British culture to make them what they were at that time. Her interpretation might have some gaps, but those are her own, formed by her understanding of her own society and its relationship with the British. This is most evident in the different responses that Taine and Krishnabhabini have towards British hospitality and affability. Taine, in quite a predicted manner, finds them most hospitable, going out of the way to help foreigners, "In the first place, I have never found the English selfish and discourteous, as they are represented to be. In London and in the country I have inquired my way hundreds of times; every one pointed it out, and several gave themselves trouble, accompanying me far enough to put me in the right path" (105). He also goes on to say that he has never encountered anyone laughing at the blunders he made in speaking English. But Krishnabhabini has a completely different experience to share. She comments on British attitude towards foreigners, "If a person's appearance differs, they stare at him as if they are staring at some beast. Sometimes even the elderly people join the children in making fun of such people and commenting derisively" (110). These differences of experience, though both correct, are also indicative of the difference in their nationalities and politics of colonialism.

Her awareness of exploitation and extortion being at the root of British prosperity is something that the Frenchman Taine, belonging to another similar imperial country cannot share. Therefore while describing the vast fleets of ships anchored or waiting near the docks of England Taine talks about the excellence and opulence of cargo brought by these vessels from various parts of the world. But Krishnabhabini points at the underlying extortion by the colonial power that aids to such overflowing merchandise in these ships. She writes,

"Stand aside and look at the boats sailing in all directions and ships waiting in queues. It seems that they have raised their heads above water to proclaim to the world the extent of British industriousness and mercantile power... None contain less than ninety to hundred maunds. Anyone looking at all these mercantile ships, assembling from all the four quarters of the world, will be amazed at the British industriousness... It sends shivers down the spines to even think of the amount of wealth these ships extort from other countries" (265).

With the direct experiences of colonial extortionist policies back home, Krishnabhabini feels the horrors while Taine is awed at the magnificence of the swelling trade and commerce of England. Though she uses Taine's figures to quantify the volume of British merchandise, she starkly differs in her analysis of the same data. This is a remarkable achievement for a Bengali woman from nineteenth century without any prior exposure to the world. It also points at her awareness regarding world politics which helps her to understand the relative position of the three countries of England, France and India. In the same passage, it is interesting to note that Krishnabhabini focuses on the 'industriousness and mercantile power' of the British, qualities which she wants her countrymen to achieve.

A close study of Taine's text also brings out a subtle competition for gaining superiority that existed among the European nations. French themselves indulged in social drinking yet Taine is quite critical of the British preference for strong liquors. There is an oblique reference to the cultural superiority of the French in the form of their predilection for lighter spirits, "our Bordeux wine and even Burgandies are too light for them" (57-58). On the other extreme is Krishnabhabini's complete abhorrence for any kind of alcohol, in keeping with the ethos of the nineteenth century Bengali middleclass society which considered drinking as one of the surest path to destruction.

Krishnabhabini not only discusses British culture, she also briefly talks about the French, particularly their women, as she crosses the French port city of Calais during her passage to England.

…(French) women are *humble and shy*. They do not belong to the *babu*[vii] class. The poor women work as hard as their husbands do—they till the fields, draw water and help their husbands in many such arduous tasks. Their faces reflect simplicity and a sense of freedom which endeared these French women to me. *I have heard that the French mothers are as caring and loving towards their children as our Indian mothers are…*The poor people too are extremely modest and I have heard that unlike the poor people of England, they do not behave like beasts after getting drunk (80). (italics mine)

The italicized portion highlights the qualities which Krishnabhabini finds lacking among the British, later in the text. She also describes Italian women and their similarities with Bengali women— "Like us, they have wide face, black hair and black eyes. Their complexion is quite fair but not pale. They seemed humble and artless, and I felt like addressing them as elder sisters" (71). Krishnabhabini comes in touch with other cultures through her brief interaction with them en route London. Taine's text also gives her a glimpse into the French culture. These together add to the cosmopolitan nature of her travel writing and help her discover many countries within Europe.

Krishnabhabini's intellectual and emotional positioning vis-à-vis the British is very different from that of Taine's. She has an important agenda behind writing her text—to make the people of her country realize their own faults and understand the virtues that make the British so powerful. Therefore, she is extremely cautious of the subjects to be included and the way to treat them. She ignores discussions on British painting and poetry though Taine spends a considerable part of his book on them. Instead, she extensively discusses women's issues. She has gone to England to learn about the traits that make British such a powerful race and therefore she focuses only on those aspects of British culture and lifestyle, ignoring the rest. Taine is not the only source that Krishnabhabini uses, though he is a major one. Krishnabhabini is familiar with texts written by both Europeans and Indians and she uses those texts along with her own understanding and experiences in England to forge a completely new one. Some of the authors who can be identified or are quoted in the text are William Makepeace Thackeray and Romesh Chandra Dutt. She also makes use of various English dailies. Apart from these there were other contemporary writings on England available which she might have read to gather information and improve her understanding of the British as a race. All these make her text a rich cultural document and help her to provide her readers with as authentic an appraisal of the British culture as possible. Taine occupies the chief place in her background research but does not at any point overshadow the persona of the Bangamahila or the Bengali lady.

Translating *Englandey Bangamahila*

Whenever a text is translated into another language, the prime intention of the translator is to make it readable to the target language readers. But the translator has to keep in mind the author's style, intention and meaning and strike a balance between the existing text in the source language and the resources available in the target language. The uniqueness of each text in terms of its location in the socio-cultural matrix demands a different approach for each. It is therefore difficult, if not impossible, to arrive at a single and perfect approach of translation. What one can possibly arrive at are various approaches to translation. Andre Lefevre and Susan Bassnett, also highlight this aspect of translation theory saying, "Translations made at different times therefore tend to be made under different conditions and to turn out differently, not because they are good or bad, but because they have been produced to satisfy different demands" (5). In fact, approach to translation varies with the translator's subjectivity as well. So, any translation at best is an approximation, a continuum which is kept alive by its very susceptibility to change as R.S Gupta says, "no two translators have ever come up with the 'same' translations of a given text or script" (190).

While translating Krishnabhabini Das' *Englandey Bangamahila* I have tried to keep my text as close to the original as possible. But given the fact that, that English and Bengali belong to two different language systems and follow very different syntax, it has not been possible to maintain a verbatim translation at all the places. My focus as a translator has been two-fold: firstly, to keep the text lucid in the target language and secondly, to be faithful as much as possible to the original author's mood, tone and cultural subjectivity as is allowed in the target language. Since English and Bengali are two languages belonging to different families and have very different syntax, a verbatim translation might result in a cumbersome sentence in English. It was a trend among the nineteenth century Bengali writers to use long and convoluted sentences unsuitable in present day English language structure. At places, therefore, I have taken some liberties with the order of the sentences. In some cases I had to break down a single sentence into a few smaller ones.

I have used the long hands of translation like footnotes and retaining in italics, the culturally untranslatable words in source language. For example, I have retained words like *sasthi puja* used by the author as it lacks an English counterpart. The word is loaded with a cultural connotation and hence, remains untranslatable in English.

Krishnabhabini Das plunges into a Sanskritised form of Bengali when she was deeply moved or awed by some scene or thing. But while translating I have not been able to maintain this difference as English language does not have much scope for it. One option could have been the use of a more stylised version of English using an archaic diction, but then again that too would have hampered readability. Therefore, in translation these passages have lost their distinctive narrative tone and have become a part of the greater narrative of the entire text.

Englandey Bangamahila also contains three poems by the author which are more personal and emotional in nature than the rest of the text. Through these poems Krishnabhabini talks about her dreams of a free country, exploitation of India by England, miserable condition of Bengali women and many such issues close to her heart. These poems are more important for their content than form. While translating them, I have therefore, primarily aimed at keeping the content intact.

These are some of the challenges faced during the translation of *Englandey Bangamahila* into English. All these challenges which a translator needs to face, invariably lead us towards the question of loss/gain in translation. The process of a dialogic intervention between the translator and the original author that opens up with every translation is in itself a 'gain' because it brings forward newer issues, previously not considered by the original author. So, at the end of every translation remains the question of how much has been sacrificed and how much has been gained in the process.

My effort has been to negotiate between the source and the target language and arrive at a negotiation between sense and semantic translation. Since, neither of these two can be used exclusively it is important to strike the right balance between them. I have tried to retain the cultural nuances which I consider is of extreme importance in a text like this where the author is deliberately comparing English and Bengali cultures. But at the same time I have tried to maintain the contemporary English diction so that the text remains easily readable to the target readers. Since the job of the translator is to make the text available to the readers who are alien to the source language and culture I have tried my best to act as the facilitator between the two language systems and interpret the culturally opaque terms to the target readers.

WORKS CITED

Bassnett, Susan and André Lefevere (Eds).*Translation, History and Culture*. London: Pinter, 1990.

Codell,Julie F. 'Reversing the Grand Tour: Guest Discourse in Indian Travel Narratives.' *Huntington Library Quaterly* 70.1 (2007): 173-189.JSTOR.Web. 12 Sept. 2011.

Das, Devendranath, *Pagoler Katha*. Kolkata: n.p. B.S. 1317.

Das, Krishnabhabini. *England-e-Bangamahila*. Calcutta: Sri Satyaprasad Sarbadhikari, 1885. Rpt. Krishnabhabini Daser *Englandey Bangamahila*. Edited with introduction by Simonti Sen, Kolkata: Stree, 1996.

—*Jeeboner Drishyamala*. Kolkata: Sri Amritlal Ghosh, B.S.1316.

Deb, Chitra. *Antahpurer Atmakatha*. Kolkata: Ananda, 1984.

Friedman, Susan. "Women's autobiographical selves: Theory and Practice". *The Private Self: Theory and Practice of Women's Autobiographical Writings*. Ed. Shari Benstock. London: Routledge, 1988. 34-62.

Gooze, Marjanne, E. "The definitions of self and form in feminist autobiography theory." *Women's Studies: An Inter-disciplinary Journal* 21.4 (1992): 411-429. JSTOR. Web. 26 June 2013.

Gupta, R.S. "Translation: A Sociolinguistic Perspective". *Translation and Multilingualism.* Ed. Shantha Ramakrishna. Delhi: Pencraft International, 1997. 183-191

Sen, Simonti. *Travels to Europe: Self and Other in Bengali Travel Narratives 1870-1910.* New Delhi: Orient Longman, 2005.

Norman, Hilda Laura. 'The Personality of Hyppolite Taine'. *PMLA* 36.4 (1921) 559-550. JSTOR 13 September, 2017.

Peyre, Henri. Review of Notes on England By Hyppolite Taine, Translated by Edward Hyams. *Victorian Studies*, 2.3 (1959) 275-277. JSTOR, 22 February, 2018.

Taine, Hippolyte. *Notes on England.* Trans. W.F. Rae. New York: Henry Holt and Co. 1885.

White John S. 'Taine on Race and Genius'. *Social Research* 10.1(1943): 76-99. JSTOR. 22 February, 2018.

A BENGALI LADY IN ENGLAND

Foreword

Readers! I am a complete stranger to you, and live hundreds of miles away; yet, I have attempted to publish a book in its present incomplete and miniature form for your pleasure. I started writing this book neither to achieve fame as an author nor to boast my knowledge. The new sights that I have come across have generated new ideas in my mind; I have tried to express them as lucidly as possible in the form of a book. My language is not exalted, the ideas presented here will not snatch away your appetite or sleep. Also, you shall not stay hooked to the book as you do while reading plays and novels. Moreover, this book does not narrate inspiring tales of heroes or heroines, or classical or tragic sagas. Here, you will only find the differences that exist between an independent life and an enslaved one. This book does not contain any speculative narration, and if you read it attentively, you might even be benefited by it. But reading it will not harm you in any way.

Nowadays, India is becoming increasingly intimate with England. The Indian youth has many queries about England before they go there; such readers also may gather some important information from this book.

My dear sisters! Like you I too was confined within my house without any knowledge about my country or the world. I had tried to be contented by knowing about a few mundane matters, but failed. I yearned to know everything about my country. I became excited, whenever, I heard someone either going to or returning from England. I craved to listen to the new experiences of that person; but unfortunately, the wishes of the subjugated women of Bengal are never fulfilled. So, I had to keep quiet. Such a curiosity regarding England might be there within you as well. I offer you this *A Bengali lady in England* to quench that thirst.

Here, I have penned down both the positive and adverse aspects of the British people according to my experiences. I have tried to present an impartial description of their lifestyle here, not taking into account the changes that occur in them when they are abroad, particularly in India. It is really difficult to be unprejudiced and critically analyse that country if we consider the differences that exist between England and India, and the kind of relationship that the British have with us. If the readers read this book with an open and balanced mind, they can appraise how successful I am in giving an unbiased account of England here.

In the course of writing this account I have consulted some English books, monthly journals and newspapers regarding certain issues. I have also consulted a few of my trustworthy British friends concerning certain customs and conducts and tried to provide a faithful account. To reduce the chances of making mistakes, I have read a few books by some British as well as some foreign authors regarding how the British judge themselves and how the people of other nations look at them. Among those, one particular book on England, written by the great French scholar Taine, has proved to be very useful. My husband had helped me generously in subjects regarding education, politics etc. He has read this book cover to cover making corrections and required changes at a number of places, and by his advice I have also included certain new issues in this draft. Without his effort and care, I could never have published this book successfully in its present form.

FROM CALCUTTA TO BOMBAY

On Tuesday, the 26th of September, at 8.30 in the evening, my husband and I reached Howrah station to leave for Bombay and from there to England. I boarded the train with my face uncovered by *ghomta*. Today, after much effort, I have prepared myself to bid farewell to my motherland and journey to England. Quietly, I took my leave from Calcutta. The bell rang, and the train along with its passengers, noisily moved ahead. Calcutta and all our kinsfolk remained behind. There were many passengers in this train, but was there any one as sad as me? Probably none. Many of them were going for a change of place[viii] or for a short trip to places like Bombay, Jabbalpur and Allahabad. They would return in a month or so and once again meet their own people. There's no reason for them to feel sad. Similarly, there's no point in talking about those who are on their way home from abroad. But was there anyone like me who was leaving her own country for a long stay in a foreign one? None I think. So my heartache could not be compared to that of anyone else's.

I started thinking of Calcutta; my childhood companion. Though, I was not born in this city, I have been staying here since my marriage. I have known her for many years; today I snapped that old bond of friendship. In a while, we crossed the stations of Hooghly, Bardhaman etc. I was already familiar with these places. Previously, when I used to visit my parents' home, I crossed these railway stations, but then, I had a veil over my face. Where is that veil today? I raised my hand to draw my ghomta, I touched the hat instead. Looking at my new attire, I felt a bit shy. Today none of my acquaintances can recognize me; they might as well salute me taking me for a memsahib. Amazing! What a great difference one's attire can make! I spent one half of the night in contemplation and the other half in dreaming. Soon it was morning again; and with day break my mind was occupied with new scenes. On our either side were stretches of lush green fields, and a few scattered huts. Half ripened harvest swayed lightly in the breeze; various kinds of birds chirped gaily as they stalked around the fields for food; herds of cows, chewing cud and tired of the scorching sun, lazed under the trees; the calves, completely oblivious to the outside world, busily suckled at their mothers' breast. Such idyllic scenes could mesmerize anyone!

We crossed newer stations. The train stopped only at the important ones and at long intervals. When it stopped at a station at around eight in the morning for about half an hour, we came out for a stroll. I felt very happy and sad at the same time. I was happy because I was free but felt sad at the same time for other Indian women who did not know the pleasure of freedom.

As the bell rang we boarded the train once again and resumed our journey. Eventually, we reached Patna. There were ruins of a few large houses near the station and the sight invoked myriad thoughts within me. In the ancient times, when the Greek king, Alexander the Great, had attacked India for the first time, Mahananda was the ruler of Magadha. He ruled from the city of Pataliputra or Patna.

This city had so much of glory and splendour then! I was shocked to see its present dreary state. There was a time when, being the capital city, it was adorned with huge buildings and forts. Now it lay quiet like any other common town.

At four in the afternoon we reached Mughalsarai. The station was terribly crowded. Later, I came to know that the crowd comprised of pilgrims, either going to Kashi (Benaras) or returning from there. Kashi, the chief pilgrimage centre for the Hindus was at a small distance from Mughalsarai. When I saw many people going to this sacred place, I too wished to go there and see this old city once again. But this wish was not fulfilled. After a short while the train started moving once more, and I kept on thinking about Kashi. Gradually, it was night. Since, I could not see anything outside, it became tedious just to keep sitting in the compartment. The train reached Allahabad at around nine-thirty at night. This was much bigger than all the other stations that we had crossed till now; besides of course, Howrah. The station was very crowded and I found that there were quite a number of British among the officials present there. Allahabad is sacred for both the Hindus and the Muslims. The city of 'Prayag', situated at the confluence of the Ganga and the Yamuna is a famous site of Hindu pilgrimage since the ancient times, and the Mussalmans also consider Allahabad as the holy city of 'Allah' or their Lord.

At Allahabad we changed our train. Here, I boarded the compartment reserved for women. There was no other woman traveller in my compartment. My husband, after assuring me enough, went to the adjacent one. I sat there all by myself. The night seemed a terrible one. Now, I was a lonely woman in an entire compartment. I had fleeting thoughts—one by one I remembered my mother, brother and sister and my heart ached. Except for a few stations and fewer lights at intervals, nothing was visible outside.

I stayed awake almost throughout the night. When it was nearly dawn, perhaps around four in the morning, I saw a light in the sky and looked out. I could see a beautiful comet. This did not seem to be the one that I had seen a few days back in Calcutta because it appeared to be bigger and brighter. It was so bright that the entire place looked illuminated by moonlight. People say that comets are ominous but, I with my limited understanding cannot comprehend how the appearance of such a pure and serene celestial object can harm this world in any way?

Slowly, sky was lit and it brightened my spirit. I shed all my worries and sat near the window to enjoy nature's beauty. At six in the morning we reached Jabbalpur. The train stopped here for about an hour. We learnt that we had to change the train once again. Many of you may know that the railway trains from Calcutta, which goes to places such as Delhi via Allahabad belongs to one particular company. The one going from Allahabad till Jabbalpur belongs to a different company and from Jabbalpur to Bombay, it is owned by still another. Many trains come directly from Calcutta to Bombay; no change is required in that case. But it was our misfortune that we could not book tickets in any such train. So we had to change our trains twice. I had heard that

Jabbalpur was a very beautiful city and its environment was congenial to one's health. Once I saw the place I realised that it was the truth. It is surrounded by hills and has wonderful scenic beauty. I wanted to stay here for a few days and visit the marvellous waterfalls of Narmada, the marble rocks and the ruins. But as our ship was about to leave for England from Bombay on the twenty-ninth of September, we could not stay back. We boarded the train immediately.

The railway station at Jabbalpur was almost as big as Allahabad and Howrah. Here majority of the staff was Marathi. I had earlier heard and read that people belonging to different regions of India have different physical features and characteristics. But having lived in Bengal, I did not actually realise it till I saw it for myself. I found the people belonging to the north-western cities such as Allahabad or Mughalsarai looking very different from the people of this place. The Marathas are shorter but they are very strong, brave and valorous. Their very appearances reveal that they are not a subservient lot. I have also heard that they are extremely clever, industrious and enduring by nature. They wear garments made of coarse cloth coupled with an *odhni* and a large turban on their heads. Most of them wear wooden shoes which look more or less like our own *kharam* or the wooden sandal, but tied to the feet with a leather or jute string. It amazes me to think of the diversity that exists within India. I contemplated that if a Bengali, a Marathi and a man belonging to the Western part of India travel abroad, none shall be able to guess that all three belong to the same country; the reasons being firstly, all three of them differ in their appearances, secondly they speak in three different languages and thirdly, the three have diverse traditions and customs. Then how could others make out that they are the sons of the same country? Again, if someone speaks to all three of them the person will find that the Bengali is clever, intelligent and educated. One can get a lot of news regarding British Empire from him and enjoy talking to him. But he is not very competent at work.

If you converse with the people of Western India, you will only get to hear the names of Lord Shiva and Goddess Durga; they are neither clever nor educated but they have strength and courage. One of their chief qualities is that they are not cunning by nature. The Marathis are not as knowledgeable as the Bengalis, but they are intelligent, diligent, quite clever and efficient in all aspects. They are also brave and spirited. They reminded me of Shivaji and other Marathi heroes. These people belong to that race of brave hearts who had tried to oust the Mughal rulers and regain India's freedom; whose weapons had killed numerous of those intruders; whose attacks were feared even by the mighty Mughal emperors and those who had ultimately brought down the Mughal Empire.

Such were the thoughts that gathered in my mind as we left Jabbalpur. From here the hilly region began. There were hillocks on either side intermitted by deep gorges and forests. The terrain was quite uneven. In Bengal, I had seen some barren hills; so I had the notion that there could not be any vegetation on hills. But here I saw hills covered with various kinds of grass, climbers and plants. It was a pleasing sight. Had I been a poet, I could have written many wonderful books in praise of its beauty. If I were a painter, I could have delighted people by my paintings of this picturesque setting. Ranges of green hills on both sides seemed to be protecting the train from all adversaries. No one could cross that barrier and harm us.

We kept moving further, and saw newer sceneries. Gradually, we reached a more mountainous region. By now, we had left the smaller hills behind and were moving through a region of higher mountains. Wherever I looked, there was an expanse of formidable mountain ranges. Towards the end of the day, nature looked all the more beautiful. As the train moved along a tributary of the river Narmada, there were green hills on one side, crystal clear water on the other and a red sky overhead. The train proceeded, sending tremors of its metallic sound all around. I wished to stop the train for a while to watch the beauty, but could not.

Gradually evening set in. I was tired after being in the train for two consecutive days and nights. Since it was almost dark and almost nothing could be seen outside, I sat quietly. Various thoughts played upon my mind. I felt happy, thinking about the diverse beauty of nature and sad at the thought of my sisters leading a life of captivity. Like me, they would have enjoyed these magnificent scenes, but unfortunately, however much they might desire, they were deprived of such happiness. As I travelled, I kept pondering over such matters. Darkness covered the entire beauty of nature. Apart from a few stations at intervals and stars in the sky, nothing was visible. Around that time we went through two big tunnels. While going through them it seemed to me that the train was fighting against the mountains, breaking through their phalanx. I was disappointed when it grew dark—why should there be night in this beautiful place? I had heard that the mountains here are really spectacular, but I could not see anything. Tomorrow, on the twenty-ninth, we shall reach Bombay and the fatigue of this train journey will be wiped away—this thought gave me some consolation. I spent the night in a state of drowsiness.

In the morning, I could see the houses, factories, and many other things around us. It seemed that overnight we had reached another world. There were no more green hills or uneven topography. As we proceeded, we saw buildings, people and factories. Factories on our either side emitted smoke. I felt elated that very soon the city of Bombay will be visible to us. Eventually, it was nine; the train reached Bombay. Porters came to take down the luggage. We got off as well. The station was crowded with people and various kinds of goods. We could not decide which way to go. My husband asked me to keep an eye on our luggage and went to arrange a hotel for our stay. Had I been standing there with my customary ghomta, so many people would have looked at me, but in our country English dresses have such an impact that no one dares to even glance this way. Everyone is scared. There were a number of hackneyed coaches in front of the station. The coachmen kept pestering me to hire one. After my husband returned, we hired one and drove to a big hotel.

Bombay is very different from Calcutta. The roads are cleaner. There are paved sidewalks along the roads, just as the ones at Chowringhee in Calcutta and the city itself appears very neat and clean. Apart from bricks, the people here also use wood and stone for building their houses. There are buildings six to seven stories high and the height of each floor is quite low. Instead of lime and mortar, the roof is covered with slate and has a slope. There is no facility for sitting or strolling on the roof. The residents here are mostly Hindu Marathis and Muslim Parsis[ix]; one can also find many people belonging to British, Eurasian or European[x] or other races. Almost all the main roads have shops on either sides and most of them are owned by the Parsis.

I think many of my native sisters do not know who the Parsis actually are. In ancient times, the people of Persia worshipped the sun and its symbol, the fire. Like us, the Hindus, they too were idol worshippers. Later, when the Muslims conquered Persia and started oppressing people to convert them to Islam, most of the Persians accepted that faith. A few of them ran away from there in an effort to save their faith and came to India seeking asylum from the King of Gujarat. The king in order to save their faith and honour granted them the permission to stay in his kingdom and also to practice their religion. Their descendants are known as Parsis today. They still follow their ancient religion as it was followed hundreds of years ago. They are clever and industrious. Wherever you see them they are always busy working and they do not understand anything apart from their work and their self-interest. They have progressed much more in business affairs as compared to Bengalis and people in other parts of India. Like China Town in Calcutta which is full of Chinese people and their shops, there are quite a few places in Bombay where there is a majority of Parsis and their shops.

In common places such as banks, post offices, schools, and colleges too they are found busy with their work and many Parsis can also be seen walking around the streets. The Parsi women are not confined like us. I have seen them on roads, stations, shops, almost everywhere. They go out in nice and decent clothes. Looking at their enthusiasm and perseverance, it does not seem that they belong to India. Wherever I go, I can see their shops or business centres. I have seen many Parsis in Calcutta but Bombay seems to be their own state. I have also heard that they own big shops in Aden, and many of them stay in London for their business. If the other communities of India emulate their qualities, then there shall be a better scope for the country's development.

Bombay is close to sea. From here it is easier to carry out business transactions with England and other European countries through the Suez Canal. The cool and healthy breeze from the sea does not let Bombay be as hot as Calcutta; perhaps that is why people are more industrious here. Bombay is not inferior to Calcutta with respect to schools, colleges, hospitals, post-offices and banks etc. I have heard that the houses, trams, horse-carriages here are somewhat like those in England; just a look would tell us that Bombay is better fitted to be the capital of British India as compared to Calcutta. England is nearer to Bombay than Calcutta. Europeans have stayed here for a longer period and possibly this makes Bombay resemble a European city.

The hotel in which we stayed was a seven storied one, built almost completely of wood and stone. It was quite well decorated, like the drawing-rooms of the rich in Calcutta. Almost all the servants of this hotel are either British or Indian Christians. The hotel is only a quarter of a mile away from the sea. Sitting in the balcony, I could see the limitless expanse of the blue sea, the bright sun overhead and the roads crowded with people and vehicles of various types. Bombay is about fourteen hundred miles away from Calcutta, after travelling this distance for two and a half days we were very tired. We wanted to rest for a while in our hotel, but heard that the ship would leave soon. After taking our meals, we left for the ship around two in the afternoon. Bigger ships could not come near the shore as it was shallow there; that is why, a couple of hours before our ship's departure, a launch or a small ship came and carried all the passengers and their luggage from the shore to the big ship.

At four in the evening, we reached the larger ship and had to climb the ladder to reach the deck. This was a new scenario for me. So many times I had seen ships from a distance, but this was the first time that I could see its interiors. The ship was full of people. On both the sides wooden ladders were placed and the people went to and fro over it; everyone was busy; trunks, letters, and sundry things were being loaded in it.

On one side I could see the city of Bombay. Hundreds of smaller boats were sailing near the shore where water was muddy and greenish. On the shore one could see both pedestrians and vehicles. There were tall white houses, standing with their necks craned towards the sea. One could keep on watching such scenes. On the other side as far as you could see, there was the vast and deep blue sea. Yet, its infinite size appeared limited by a boundary of ships at a distance. All these together gave a feeling that there were some houses full of people floating on the sea. I could not decide which way to gaze at. There were boats and people around our ship, almost all the people were Parsis, Muslims or Christians. It seemed that we had bid farewell to the Hindus on the shore itself.

I did not know if ever I would see Bombay again; neither did it seem probable that I shall return to India. Thinking of these I came to the side of the ship overlooking the shore and kept watching. Thoughts of leaving India, the land of my birth and my home for so many years, as well as pangs of leaving my friends and kin made me restless. There was no end to the crowd of people. Gradually, it was six in the evening and I realised that the ship had not yet set sail. Just then there was a siren to alert people that the ship would leave in another fifteen minutes. People, other than the passengers, finished their jobs quickly and started disembarking. Within ten minutes almost three-fourth of the people had left the ship leaving only the passengers and the crew on it. There was another siren shortly—now the ship started moving.

FAREWELL

Oh my dear country! My *swadesh*—the jewel!
Leaving you for a long time.
Oh ma! Do not anymore
think of this hapless daughter,
she could not be of any help.

There was a hope that with my beloved
 I shall work for your upliftment!
 Yet, that desire remains unfulfilled,
 lying dormant within myself.

That hope's slowly fading away.
But, oh ma! Memory remains,
like a poison hidden in my heart
and causes pain.

I still have no answer
to your question
of our reasons for leaving India!
Yet we are going abroad
with many hopes in our hearts.

Since many days I have nurtured
a secret wish—to meet dear Freedom,
in the country where she lives.

I shall go to that place
where the goddess of Freedom
resides in every hearth;
where everybody is happy
and all live in peace.

Oh mother! There is no chain of bondage
around the necks of human beings.
The sons of England enjoy happiness
which is the gift of freedom.

I ardently wish to know why England,
so respected, civilized and well educated
is so deluded as to oppress
India and make her miserable.

FROM BOMBAY TO VENICE

The ship left on Friday, around 6:30 in the evening: within the whole gamut of play, curtain rose to introduce a new scene of my life. I was leaving India for the first time. As the ship kept sailing further, my heart grew heavier. It was not because I was afraid of the sea; instead, it gave me a new kind of thrill. But this pain was heart wrenching. India is my birthplace and I have lived here for all these years. I love her with my entire soul. Looking at her down trodden condition, I blamed myself for being unable to do anything for her.

I was not sure for how long I was going to be away from our dear land. With a lot of nerve I had steadied myself but a surge of grief swept away my brave front. There were tears in my eyes but I could not cry. I was conscious of being discovered crying by others and tried to divert myself. But how could I do so? I had cherished my beloved motherland for so many years; how could I forget her so easily? I kept thinking of all my relatives, wanted to get off the ship, and run away. Then I remembered the history books that I had read. I used to hate the cowards who got scared and ran away from battlefields; so if I quit, it would be an act of extreme cowardice and people would hate me for not being strong-willed. Thus arguing with myself and with a lot of effort, I took my leave from India. The ship moved ahead. Why are the people of our country so scared of ships? Here I found so many passengers, and they were neither troubled nor anxious.

Talking of danger—well, danger is present everywhere. You can die of an illness at your home or can even die of lightning. But, if the ship sinks then you will die by drowning—this is the only difference. Gradually it was evening; it appeared new to me.

There was Bombay—still visible, though you could not see anybody in particular or get any clear impression. But I could see some houses painted white. One by one all the lights were being switched on, and they were visible through the windows of those houses. We were still within the bay of Bombay. On three sides there was the city with its tall buildings that appeared like saints in white robes meditating on the shore while the waves washed their feet. At times, the waves were dancing around to disturb the meditating saints but they were so deeply immersed in their prayers that they did not get bothered. Slowly, dense darkness engulfed the world. Stars appeared in the sky. I looked at the city, which seemed to be wearing a garland of stars. I looked towards the sea again—friction between the ship and the water at times made phosphorous glow like stars. It seemed that we were sailing through the infinite sky.

All the lights of Bombay gradually faded away. I looked around to check whether any of those were visible— but no, I could not find any. I tried again but failed. Within this last hour we had lost the sight of Bombay. There was a void in my heart as I felt moving away from my country, India. I was leaving *swadesh* today—that *swadesh* for which people travelled hundreds of miles to return to her. It was that land which the people yearned for even when they lived abroad; and it was that *swadesh* which no one wanted to leave. I did not know when I would get to see her again. When all these thoughts were troubling me, I suddenly saw a light at a distance. I felt very happy thinking that Bombay was not completely lost till then. When I asked my husband about it, he said that this light was not from Bombay. There were lighthouses built near certain shores for the convenience of the ships. This light belonged to one of those. It brightened and dimmed alternately reflecting my state of mind. I was surprised. Standing in this silent, deep sea, was it shivering out of fear?

No, perhaps it was neither coward nor weak like a Bengali woman. Had it been scared like us, how could it stand in the sea, alone and resolute, and show way to the mariners? I heard that it glows alternately because of a rotating mirror like glass, fitted at its top. When light falls on that glass, it glows as brightly as the sun. The lighthouse from a distance looked like a pillar; I have heard that it closely resembles the monument of Calcutta. There are stairs inside it and at the top there is a big circular room containing the light. There is a room downstairs in which a man stays. Every evening he lights that lamp. He is in complete charge of the lighthouse.

We were very tired; so we went to bed as soon as it was night. The ship swayed gently but, I felt neither uneasy nor giddy. Many people suffer from dyspepsia on ship, they cannot eat anything and even if they do, they immediately throw up. I have heard that this seasickness is as agonizing and weakening as vertigo. Some people get cured in a few days but, many take a long time to get well. There are perhaps only a handful of voyagers who are not affected by this. It is difficult to find the reason behind this. There is always a mild swaying of the ship and it increases if the wind is stronger. Firstly, many people cannot tolerate this swaying. The high salt content in the water and air of the ocean makes people suffer from digestive disorders. To add to it, extremely foul smelling oil is used in the machine rooms and at other places of the ships. Perhaps all these together cause seasickness. Surprisingly, children are almost never affected. I had not slept for the last three nights and thought that, I would get a deep sleep now. But for some time my sleep remained disturbed by various thoughts. After a while I fell asleep. Thus was my first night in the ship.

I woke up at six in the morning. Just then a 'steward' knocked at our door and my husband got up to take our tea and biscuits from him. I left my bed and had some of those; thereafter I went to the 'deck'. Now there was only the sea all around, neither the city nor houses were visible—it was blue everywhere. Not a bird flew in the sky. If one looked towards the sea, one could see just the waves, each following the previous one even before it broke—one after the other. But these waves were not very big ones. The sea was almost calm now except a mild stir, disturbed as if by the ship.

There were not many passengers in this ship; twenty-five people in the first class and only fourteen in the second. The vessel was neither very big, nor very small; it was about twelve and a half yards long and seven and a half yards in breadth. In a ship, the topmost part is called 'deck'. It has no covering. When there is too much of heat or rain, the sail is used as cover. On the deck there are the captain's room, kitchen, and some small machines here and there in between. Downstairs, on one side there are small rooms like those in a train, known as cabins, and a big, well-decorated room for the first-class passengers, to sit and dine. It is called 'salon'.

All the cabins are not of the same size, each containing two, four or more number of beds. The beds are arranged in a tier system, and often, to reach the top most berths, the person has to almost wrestle with oneself. When I first entered the cabin, I did not think it would be possible to spend the night in that pigeonhole. Raising your hand, you could touch the roof and the beds were so narrow that I thought the Goddess of Sleep would never grace me there. Anyway, gradually I adjusted to everything. If you think logically, you would realise that a better arrangement than this was not possible in a ship. On those walls of the cabins which faced the sea, there were small windows like the air holes that we see in our country. Those are called 'port-holes'. Apart from those there were a few more cabins with excellent arrangement for bathing and other facilities.

At one end of the ship there are cabins for the first-class passengers as well as the officers, and at the other end, there are cabins for the second-class passengers and seamen. In the central part of the ship there is a machine room with a huge engine that propels the ship to move. It is very hot there and the roar of the engine combined with foul smelling oil made it difficult for anyone to stand there for long. Just below our cabin there were two to three very big cases, or the ship's hold, in which the cargo that the ship carried and the bigger trunks of the voyagers were kept. The base of the ship lay beneath the hold.

The person at the head of the ship, known as 'captain', had four subordinates. These five people, in accordance to their order took charge of the ship. But the captain was the overall in-charge of the ship. There were six engineers to look after the entire machinery of the ship and a doctor on board to treat any person falling ill. Every Sunday, a church was organized in which the doctor or the captain functioned as the priest. Under them there were four other men called 'quarter master'. They carried out the orders of the captain and his subordinates. Those who worked as servants in the ship were known as 'stewards'.

The chief steward was responsible for food. He decided the menu, its quantity etc and supervised everything like a mistress of the house. All the other stewards served food, made the beds, washed utensils etc. There were sixteen stewards in all, and a 'stewardess' for all the women travellers. There were people for almost all types of jobs—three to four cooks, barbers, carpenters, blacksmiths etc. There were about six Africans employed to work in the machine-rooms near the fire. They could bear extreme heat. In our ship there were around sixty sailors from Bombay engaged in chores such as cleaning the ship, unfurling the sail, anchoring the ship etc.

Soon it was noon. The sun grew brighter causing the sea to sparkle. The waves rose and fell gracefully playing with the rays of the sun. The captain and a couple of his crew adjusted the time in keeping with the position of the sun. It was two o' clock at the very time when it showed quarter to two the previous day. As we moved along, time differed by a quarter of an hour. I wanted to sit on the deck and read. But that was not possible; I felt drowsy, the swaying ship seemed to lull me into sleep. Upon the deck it was a scorching sun but tempered by a cool breeze. I held the book in my hand and sundry thoughts came to my mind—one by one I thought about India, my birthplace, Calcutta, friends and relations. Everyone there would be in exactly the same condition as when I had left them. But in the four days I had travelled a great distance and undergone a huge change in my food habits and things! If my mother could see me now, she would have cried thinking that I have converted into a Christian, my brothers and sisters would not rush towards me and dare to call me *didi* loudly or hold my hands lest they become outcastes too. Other relatives would tease me and call me memsahib. But there had been no change within me. I did not have the customary *ghomta*, a must for a Hindu wife. I had become so British in my eating habits and attire that no one would recognise me as a daughter of a Hindu. Yet, I had the same love towards my mother, father, brother, sister and other relations. If I could meet them, I would have hugged them and talked to them. I still felt the same longing for India. Some Indians bring false allegations that the moment an Indian boards a ship, the person changed. I think they say so because they believe that difference in attire brings in a change in the nature as well.

Gradually the sun lost its brightness. At the time of sunset the sky looked red, and the sea seemed to be on fire with flames leaping up to the sky. I had seen sunsets many a times in India but none looked so fascinating. My surrounding was not just blue any more. Looking at the reddish sky overhead, I thought we were near some human habitat. I felt as excited as that traveller who, lost in the darkness of night, sees the lights of a distant city. The sun moved farther from us gradually. I could see half of it and then it disappeared completely. The sky was still red. The sun had left its light behind. Even after the sunset, its glow bespoke of its greatness, just as, fame betokens the great deeds of a saint even long after his death. Slowly darkness engulfed everything. Once again the sky was deep blue. Now, the blue moonlit sky was studded with thousands of stars, and the moon situated amidst them radiated its soothing light.

If you observe the sea—you would see thousands of moons dancing upon the waves, swaying for a while before disappearing. Oh! What a sight! Sitting on the deck I kept watching the stars and wondered whether these were the same stars that I could see from India? I had come such a long way from India, could I get a glimpse of those same stars from here as well? Oh look! Those are our well-known planets – Venus and Mars and our familiar Big Dipper, Orion and other constellations shining brightly in the sky. I felt glad to locate the known stellar bodies in the sky here. We used to sit together on the terrace of our house in Calcutta and watch them. The stars are here, still visible to me but where are the other people? Would I meet them ever again?

Next morning, I woke up to find the sea still as a pond. I opened the porthole to have a look. I was bored after a while. Just as the bell rang I changed quickly and went for breakfast. In the ship, a bell was rung before each meal. On finishing breakfast, we once again went to the deck to watch the sea. But it was the same sky, same people; everything was just the same. Now life in the sea appeared dreary. Had my husband not been with me during this voyage, I would have faced a tough time because he was the only one I could talk to. There were other women on board, but we did not have much conversation with them. I have heard that when the British go to India from England, they are polite towards the Indians and treat them as equals but when they are on their way back, they strike a different attitude. Their politeness disappears. Therefore I too did not talk to anyone.

Six days passed in this way. When I went to the deck on Friday morning, I saw something like smoke at a distance; gradually as we went nearer, it appeared like a shore. I felt an indescribable pleasure. Only one who has spent six to seven days continuously in water can understand this happiness. There was a time when I longed to see the ocean, and now I was restless for land. Gradually, as the land approached, I became more cheerful. Around ten o'clock in the morning we approached Aden. There was a siren to inform us that we had reached the port. Sailors hurried to anchor the ship that had come to a halt.

Aden was quite close by. There were white and red houses in the lap of black and grey hills, behind which were the roads and beyond them, the sea again. It seemed that Aden had risen out of the sea. Along the road there were small but very strong dikes built to keep the waves at bay. Loking towards one side I found a number of small boats near the ship. Ladders were let down from both its sides, and many new people were climbing on board. Most of them were peddlers of various kinds. Some people showed us large feathers, others asked us to buy ornaments. At another place I saw a Persian sitting with many kinds of toys. Going to the edge of the ship I saw another new scene; about twenty-five to thirty small boys, each on a small dinghy were shouting 'oho, have a dive' and asking for money. If a coin was thrown in the water, they would immediately dive into the sea and effortlessly find it out. One of them said that, if someone threw the coin to the other side of the sea, he could swim under the ship and retrieve it. I threw a two *anna* coin to test him and I saw that he dived and picked it up. But I could not understand whether he went along the side of the ship or swam underneath it. Anyway, due to their talent in swimming these boys resembled some kind of aquatic creatures[xi]. They did not seem to ever grow taller and all of them looked alike—very dark complexioned with thick growth of sand coloured hair. They looked like Africans. The people here spoke Arabic but since the British, French, and other races frequently visited this place, they knew a smattering of all those languages including Hindustani. Thus, they had a working knowledge of all these languages.

Everyone knows that Aden is under British rule. It is of a great importance to the British because they have to cross this place while going to India. They pamper Aden a lot. Many people describe this place as the gateway to India. This is the reason for which the British have built a fort in this desert and have posted a troop of soldiers there. Since there is a very close contact between Aden and India, the British considers it as a part of the Bombay presidency. Almost all the ships on their way stop here for eight to ten hours to replenish their stock of coal. In the mean time, the passengers go to the shore for sight-seeing.

At twelve noon we took a boat to the shore. The sea-shore had miles of sand and there were a few shops owned by some Persian and British people, about two to three hotels, a post-office, etc. We took a car and visited the city. There was not much to see except a few tanks or ponds. Nobody knows who had built these tanks. It is said that many years ago, when this place was ruled by the Arabs, these deep tanks had been dug to store rain water and save people from drought.

Now, no one takes care of these any more. The land here is very barren and sandy; we could not see green fields or trees anywhere. Here camels carry all types of loads; some horses and horse carts are also available. Houses in Aden are very similar to the ones we have in Bengal, many among which are made of stone. In spite of the sea breeze blowing, the weather is very hot. Add to that the scarcity of drinking water. Perhaps that is why no one wants to stay here. But many people have to somehow spend their lives here on account of their jobs. In Aden, there are Arabians, Africans, Jews, Indians, British, French, and people from other races. Here population is scarce; apart from the soldiers, almost everyone is engaged in business. The various streams of commerce that flow through the four continents meet in

Aden. The ships coming from India, China, Australia, Japan, South Africa, go via Aden to Europe or America.

On returning to the ship again at three in the afternoon, we found it to be extremely crowded and covered with coal-dust. They bring coal in boats from the shore, which is then loaded into the ship. This takes about three to four hours, and during this time, coal dust settles on all the things around turning them black. The doors and windows of the rooms are kept shut and it becomes difficult for people to remain on board. Within a couple of hours the sailors cleaned up everything. When all the outsiders had left, the ship blew its siren, it was a signal to leave. Looking towards the port of Aden, you could see a number of ships sailing—red, black, blue and white—with their own flags fluttering in the air! All the ships belong to the Europeans, and most of them are owned by the British; there were no ships belonging either to the Indians or to any other Asian country. After two or three ships left, we also started moving. While darkness spread, we lost sight of Aden.

The next morning, we woke up to find that we had reached the Red Sea. I had thought that the Red Sea would appear red. But like the Indian Ocean this one was also blue. Here in the month of *ashwin* the weather was as hot as our *jesth*[xii]. The Red sea is not very wide; it was particularly narrow for quite a stretch from the port of Aden. Here we did not feel as though we were in the middle of a sea. On the two sides we could see the shores of Arabia and Africa. Gusts of searing hot air were blowing from time to time from the deserts of these two places. The ocean here was quite dangerous; there were a number of hillocks under the surface of water. Therefore, the ship had to be steered very carefully through these regions.

I had heard that the Red Sea got its name because a number of people had lost their lives here. Today, the captain was very busy. Instead of allowing his crews to steer the ship, he was doing it himself. He did not have the time to eat as well. The sun was very bright in the morning and the night sky was absolutely clear. The stars and planets were shining brightly and their lights fell on water to illuminate the place. Actually, I had never seen such a sky in India. Here I saw another new scene. When I was in India, I had heard of a fish that could fly; here I saw the real flying fish. They could not fly continuously like birds, but from time to time, they flew a few feet above the sea level, like ducks. They were white with a reddish tinge and glittered under the sunshine.

A few more days passed as I enjoyed these scenes. On Tuesday, around eight in the evening, I saw a light at a distance. Many people observed it through telescopes but none could identify its source. Some said that it was another ship; others thought it to be light from the city of Suez. After about half an hour, when some more lights were visible, we realised that we were near the city of Suez. The ship stopped after some time. I had thought that we would take a train from Suez to Alexandria, and from there we would reach Brindisi by a ship. But that was not to be. All mails between India and England had to pass through this route but this time even that was not allowed; the reason being, the war in Egypt. Though the war had actually ended by then and that route had been reopened, none of the passengers were allowed to get down lest there be some trouble. Therefore, we had to go through Suez Canal, covering the entire journey by water. Ships are not allowed in the canal at night, so we spent the night at the port. The city of Suez was about four miles away, but since it was already dark, nothing was visible. I kept looking at the lights as long as I could, thereafter, feeling tired, went off to sleep.

The next morning, I woke up to see a number of small boats and many people on both sides of the ship. There were ships of different colours and types in the port. I had never seen so many ships at one place. It was just a few days that the war was over. A number of ships were still waiting there. There were two or three different flags unfurled at the top of each ship. The flags either showed the race of the owner of the ship or the company to which it belonged. I could see white coloured houses at a distance. And I saw busy people nearby—getting up, climbing down, coming here, or going away—I felt like going and joining them. Those ships, which were waiting in the canal at night, came out one by one and the ships which were in the port, started moving towards the canal. This went on till twelve noon. At one o'clock our ship left post to slowly enter the canal.

The canal was so narrow that more than one ship could not pass. If the ship sailed fast, then soil from both the banks might slide and choke the canal itself: so the ship had to move very slowly. At some intervals in the canal there were stops similar to railway stations. Near those stations, the canal was wider. So if two ships came together, at these places, one was made to stop while the other moved on. Gradually, we left the city of Suez behind.

Now, there were open spaces on either side of the canal, most of it being sandy desert. There were a few houses far from each other. Apart from these, nothing else was visible. The ship was moving very slowly. It had to halt for a number of times in between and stopped completely at night. So we had to spend two nights before covering much of a distance. Later, we reached a lake. Since the canal merged with the lake here, this place was much wider, so the ship moved a bit faster here. At eleven o'clock in the morning, we reached the city of Ismailia. The ship stopped. Here a few boats approached the ship but since no ladder was lowered, none of them could come on board. They started selling eggs, fish, fruits, from their boats itself. The fruits were delicious, here I tasted fresh pomegranate, such succulent grapes, apples and some other kinds of fruits that I had never seen before. My eyes had grown tired of watching water and fields only. Now, looking at the white houses and green trees, I felt very happy. There is a royal palace in Islamia where the khedive of Egypt comes and stays at times.

By now we had crossed almost half of the canal. We left Ismailia and proceeded further. Next day, we crossed a number of ships on our way, and when I saw one of them going to Calcutta, my mind wavered. I would have been too happy to be in that ship; or any Indian on that ship, on his way back to his own country must be happy too! The pain of yearning for one's own country can only be felt by those who are living abroad.

Suez Canal is about ninety miles long and for about seventy miles, its width is about 54.5 yards and for the rest of the 18 miles, it is only 32.5 yards wide. The work of digging this canal began in the year 1860 and was completed in 1869. The idea of Suez Canal was first thought of by a famous French person, Monsieur Ferdinand de Lesseps and now we are enjoying this fruit of his intelligence and efforts. Around twenty-two crores of rupees has been spent in its construction, apart from that there was the cost of the land and the Khedive of Egypt had forced many workers to work on it without any payment.

Earlier, the route to India through the south of Africa was about 11000 miles, after the construction of this canal it has been reduced to only 7400 miles and this route has reduced the span of journey by thirty-six days as compared to the previous one. It is documented that in the year 1877, 1651 ships had crossed this canal among which 1291 belonged to the British. In that year, the revenue earned from this canal was around 16000000 rupees and since then it has only increased. It is maintained by a French company. Monsieur Lesseps is their leader and their main office is in Paris, the capital of France. All those ships which take this route have to pay to this company according to the quantity of their cargo.

On Friday evening, at seven o' clock our ship crossed the canal and reached the city of Port Said. We felt relieved. If a ship moves at a constant speed, the canal can be crossed in ten hours, but as it moved slowly, halting a number of times, it took us two and a half days. Port Said too was extremely crowded with ships. Since it was night, they were not properly visible, only their lights gleamed. From a distance it looked like a floating diamond necklace. There were a number of shops on the sea-shore which looked charming in their bright lights. These shops were quite attractive to the passengers of the ship. But as it was night, none ventured to the shore. I have heard that Port Said is a dangerous place, all the notorious people from various European countries gather there.

The ship in which we were sailing would reach England via south of Europe, but we and a few other passengers wanted to go to England through Europe via Italy and so we left this ship and embarked a different one. This new ship was a bit smaller than the previous one, but cleaner and taller. Apart from three or four of us there was no other Indian in it; the sailors were all Italian and the captain and his crew were British. The ship sailed within half an hour. Finally we were leaving Asia behind. The thought grieved me. Leaving Port Said would mean cutting off all relations with Asia. Till Port Said one doesn't feel very far from India because the people and their houses in Aden, Suez or Port Said keep reminding us of that place. But from here on, everything would be different and the farther you go, you would come across more Europeans, and find many new things.

By the time we woke up the next day, we had reached the Mediterranean Sea. Here too, like in the Indian Ocean we could see only blue water all around and blue sky above. On Monday, as we moved ahead we saw the small hills in islands near Greece. There was no end to the sea; if we felt so restless in just a few days in the sea, think how much those people who had to spend one and a half years, or nine months, or six months or three months, during their passage between England and India had to suffer. Tuesday, early morning, we were within four miles of Brindisi, a town in the south-east of Italy. But what a luck! In spite of Brindisi being so near, we could not disembark the ship. The Italians did not allow us to visit that place lest cholera enters Europe, particularly Italy, from Egypt. Such an arrangement is called 'quarantine'. This rule is very strictly followed. When cholera breaks out in India or Egypt, they detain the ship for ten, fifteen or even twenty-five days and do not let it keep any kind of contact with the shore.

Brindisi was just ahead. White coloured houses were visible at a distance and nearby there were the masts of ships. A couple of Italian ships crossed us to reach the port, but we kept sitting like prisoners, unable to move about. At seven o' clock in the morning a doctor and two superintendents from the Italian government came to check all of us for cholera and other diseases. Everyone on board had to go to them. None of us were suffering from any disease; still no one was allowed to get off the ship before spending three days near the port, or in areas near Italy. They only took letters packed in gunny sacks, and those too very carefully. Everyone felt irritated at this unnecessary wastage of time, but we were helpless. Instead of keeping the ship in the port for three days, the captain started moving northwards, towards Venice. We reached the Adriatic Sea and kept sailing along the eastern coast of Italy.

On Wednesday, when we saw a number of fishing boats, we realised that we were near some human habitation. Slowly Venice was visible to us from a distance. Here again the ship came to halt. Everyone was eager to go to Venice, but as it was not yet three days since we left Brindisi, we were not allowed to. Everyone started criticizing the Italian government. It was not a foreign dominated country such as India that the British could do whatever they felt like. This was a free country; here no other country could establish its stronghold. In this way we spent another day here. On Thursday morning we sailed again. We kept moving towards Venice through a canal. There were small islands on the two sides, green trees at intervals, various types of houses of white and red colours and then again water. Almost around eight at night we reached Venice. We heard that next morning once again a doctor, now from Venice, would visit the passengers; irritated, I went to my cabin.

Next morning at six, a doctor belonging to the Italian government came to give a medical check up to the people on board. None in the ship was found ailing. It was three days in the sea since our departure from Brindisi, we felt very happy as now we would be free to leave the ship. The ship anchored near the shore. Many small boats came near the ship. These boats are called Gondola here. They look similar to the dinghy of our country. We started preparations for disembarking the ship, meanwhile a few people from the Italian excise department arrived and started checking all our luggage. While travelling in a foreign country one has to pay a duty for a number of things, the duty on tobacco is particularly high. If one possesses it in a quantity more than his personal requirement and keeps it hidden without paying the tax, then if caught, the person might be fined or punished. After all these were over, on 18th October, at eight-thirty in the morning we took a gondola to Venice.

FROM VENICE TO LONDON

First we took a gondola to the railway station of Venice. Contrary to our expectations, there was no respite from the sea even here, it appeared endless. Charting our way through a number of canals, we reached the station. Upon reaching, we found that no one knew English, all spoke Italian and a few could speak French. Thankfully, my husband knew French, so we could somehow manage. We learnt that our train would depart at eleven o' clock at night. We took another boat from the station and once again, crossing a number of canals of various sizes, we reached a hotel. There we had something to eat and then went out on a tour of the city. This was my first step on any European land. I cannot express my curiosity and the happiness that filled my heart while touring through Italy.

Venice is situated in the northeastern corner of Italy. It is an interesting city; one cannot find another place similar to it. It consists of a group of islands. At a glance, it seems that a number houses are floating on the ocean. Just as other cities have roads, they have canals. If you want to go from one place to another, you can find a number of boats at your doorstep; you can hire one and travel. There are rows of houses along the sides of the canals and overhead bridges in between. There is silence, as there is no noise from any vehicle. While in other cities the rich own cars or horses, here they own gondolas and boatmen. I did not see any horse or vehicle in this city. One can also walk around in this city along the bridges, but there are high bridges after every five minutes and one has to climb a number of stairs. So it is quite inconvenient to travel like this. I have heard that in the ancient times, there was an Italian king who was a great lover of ocean. He wished to build a house over the sea. He is the creator of this city on sea.

Beside our hotel was the Saint Mark Square, which looked like a paved courtyard. There were fine shops of various products along the four sides of the square. They were so beautifully decorated that it was difficult to take eyes off them. We went to an ordinary garden and found it crowded with people, mostly women; all the people—the poor or rich, women and men—were strolling or sitting and talking among themselves. Looking at them, I was reminded of my sisters in India who were leading a confined life, and felt very sad; they could not even think of such happiness. Women of this country are mostly good-looking. Like us, they have wide face, black hair and black eyes. Their complexion is quite fair but not pale. They seemed humble and artless, and I felt like addressing them as elder sisters. But unfortunately, we could not talk to them as we could not speak Italian. I had read that the Italian women were not very well educated, but they did not appear stupid. There was a mark of culture and freedom visible upon their visage.

The day ended, we returned to our hotel and had dinner. Then, after a short nap we went to the station at ten o' clock at night and boarded the train for London. I felt happy thinking that our journey would end in another few days. Somehow the night passed. Next morning, as we travelled we watched the northern part of Italy. It seemed to me that though Venice appeared richer than any of our cities, Italy was a poor country. It reminded me of India.

Even now one can find certain traces which prove that the Italians and Indians have a lot in common. Even now the poor women here use scarves instead of hats, similar to our ghomta and many of them wore long skirts and shirt, like those worn by the women of north-western India. The civilizations of the ancient Hindus and Italians belonged to the same period, both the races were idol worshippers, and there were many similarities between their customs and costumes. Italians have undergone a lot of changes since then—customs, tradition, religion, attire, everything has completely changed. Italy went through a dire phase after the fall of the Roman Empire. They did not just lose their name and prestige, but also their freedom, busy fighting among themselves. After a number of years, when they gradually became aware of their faults and their degenerated condition, they finally resolved their differences and regained their freedom with the help of famous patriots like Mazzini, Garibaldi and others. But what has happened to our India? One of our Indian poets in an answer to this has truly said— 'India keeps on just sleeping'.

Around eight in the morning we reached Milan and took another train to go towards Switzerland. A short while after leaving Milan we reached the mountainous region. Such a wonderful beauty of nature! I was impressed by the sight of the mountain ranges in Jabbalpur on our way from Calcutta to Bombay, but the inimitable and inexpressible natural beauty that I saw here was beyond my imagination, beyond my dreams.

On either side of us were the high mountains standing with their heads held up to the sky. In between there were fountains from which water gurgled out, disturbing the serenity of this tranquil place. At a distance this water took the form of a rapidly flowing brook. At other places, this water accumulated in greater quantity to form a pond. Not very far from this place were the vast valleys, dark due to their cover of green grass and trees. At some places cows, horses and other such animals could be seen while at other places there were a few houses. Everything looked doubly bright and beautiful under the sun. There was complete silence except the sound made by the train moving at a great speed. Wow! So much of difference in nature! At every moment there was something new to see. The train was moving through the plateau region of this mountain. After a while we started descending again. The train descended at a great speed, it seemed to me that the entire world was rushing downwards from a sky-high mountain. Those, which looked like leaves from a distance, appeared to be trees on approaching and those which looked like small brooks, later turned out to be broad rivers. There were mountains after mountains and the further we proceeded, we could see more and more amazing scenes. Nature gradually turned sombre. Ahead of us I could see another huge mountain. I thought that now the train would stop, but eventually, it entered the mountain and passed through it. We crossed a number of similar tunnels at a great speed.

We reached a valley in the northern corner of Italy. Here we came across another new scene. Suddenly nature became quite serene. We had left the mountains behind. There were a few ahead of us but they were too far to be clearly visible. Entire area was covered with different kinds of trees, climbers, etc. with a beautiful, large lake nearby. There were a few white houses around the lake. Men and women were happily strolling along its sides, small girls and boys were playing and ducks and other water creatures were happily swimming. It was already the season of *sharat*[xiii], but in this country where winter predominates, the flora had not yet lost brightness. In the gentle breeze, flowers swayed lightly to entertain nature. Swaying lightly in the gentle breeze, the flowers appeared to be entertaining nature. A bit farther, one or two farmers were working. Terrible winter had not set in yet to make the earth barren. There were some clouds in the sky and their shadow on the clean and quivering water of the lake added to its beauty. This was the beginning of the month of *Kartik*[xiv], but the sun was less scorching; and though it was afternoon, a cool and soothing breeze was blowing. I felt drowsy reflecting upon nature's exquisite beauty. For a while I fell asleep.

I woke up all of a sudden and saw that we had reached a very dark and mountainous region. On both sides, there were two huge and barren mountains; however high I might look up, I could not see the tip of its peak. Never in my life had I seen such tough and horrible looking mountains. There was no trace of greenery. Large chunks of stones were falling on the plateaus and I was scared that very soon they would crush our bones. There were some caves in these mountains gaping at us, but even the sun's rays could never reach here. At places there were high waterfalls making loud noise as they fell from high mountains with a great force. Along with that there were echoes of the noise from various vehicles. These noises assaulted our ears. What a disturbance in nature that in such a secluded place there should be so much of a noise! Looking closely I saw that we were moving across a very narrow bridge. Far beneath us was the plain land. I felt nervous to see downwards.

Gradually, as we gained altitude we started feeling cold. Since we did not have any warm clothing we wrapped ourselves with whatever we had and kept the windows of our carriage shut. But the awe and delight with which we watched the picturesque beauty of nature made us forget everything else. By then, we had reached the foothills of the Alps. All the earlier views of nature appeared trivial. Nature's bounty; its grandeur left us speechless. We kept staring upwards. We saw continuous ranges of peaks overlapping each other. The foothills were covered with various strange plants, but as we went higher, these plants became scarce. At a greater altitude, nothing green was visible. One could only see naked brown stones. There were snow-capped high peaks which sparkled when sun's rays fell upon them. From a distance it looked like the king of the mountain wearing his crown of diamonds. It was the first time that we saw snow; I cannot justly express how astonished and delighted I was by such a view. At places spring water sloped down the back of the mountain through paths resembling a white intricate plait or when its movement was obstructed by some rocks, it splashed water droplets all around. Sun rays shone upon these droplets and created beautiful rainbows. Elsewhere, there were large stretches of desert like areas along the mountain slopes. There were certain areas that seemed completely inaccessible by any kind of living organisms.

Watching such overwhelming beauty of nature and reflecting upon the inconceivable power of our Creator and His unparalleled creation, we moved ahead. These miraculous scenes were actually proof of His greatness and power. We reached very close to the peak of Saint Gotthard in the Alps range. There was a huge, incredible mountain looming ahead of us. Its grave demeanour asked us to stay away from it, lest our proximity desecrated it. I thought that here was mankind's defeat by nature; he would not be able to cross this insurmountable mountain. But thanks to man's knowledge and intellect he had succeeded in building tunnels through this impenetrable Alps with the help of science and technology. We went through these tunnels and crossed Italy to reach Switzerland.

The station was just beside the tunnel. We came to know that the train would stop there for half an hour. We got down the train and after our meals, took a walk around that place. Just ahead was the lofty mountain and the tunnel below looked no more than a small hole. We had crossed the terrible mountain; I wondered whether there was anything impossible for man! I mulled over the tunnel. On one of its side was a small town of Italy, named Airolo, while on the other side was Göschenen, a Swiss village. The length of the tunnel was almost ten miles and it was only twenty-two and half feet wide, only two vehicles could move alongside at a time. It took us forty-five minutes to cross it. Once inside, we could not see anything, as it was completely dark. Apart from the sound of the train, nothing else could be heard.

Italy and Switzerland together had begun the construction of this tunnel in the year 1872 and it was completed by 1881. Initially, the expense for the construction of this tunnel was estimated to be about nine crore rupees, but by the time the construction was over, it went upto fifteen crores. There is another similar tunnel through the Alps joining Italy and France called Mont Cenis tunnel. It is smaller than Saint Gotthard tunnel but, it required more ingenuity and technical skills. Musing about the knowledge and intelligence of the European engineers, we boarded the train again at four o' clock in the afternoon.

We started moving through the hilly regions of Switzerland. All around us there were mountain ranges, similar to those which we had crossed earlier; the train moved, sometimes over the mountains, sometimes through them or at other times along their sides. I looked back but the high peak of Saint Gotthard was not visible anymore. The rail track was serpentine, if at one moment we were atop a mountain, the next moment we reached its foot. I could not help thanking the European engineers when I thought of the amount of skill and effort that had gone into building a railway through such impassable and rugged terrain. Also, we could move so fast as a result of this motor vehicle. In the morning, we were in Italy while by evening we had reached

Switzerland. There we heard people speaking in a particular language and in Switzerland they spoke another completely different one. We progressed further watching the scenery of Switzerland.

Soil in that region was quite fertile due to the fountain which gave rise to many streams and lakes on its either side. This country experiences severe cold—winter lasts for almost eight months a year. This year snowfall had started by early *Kartik*. Yet, there was a variety of flora here in its valley. At places, there were big trees whose green, leafy branches swayed gently in the evening breeze—it was a very pleasing scene. Here most of the houses were built of stone and some were made of wood. They had slanting roofs and big chimneys atop each of these. When I looked at these white houses from the train, I felt like leaving the train and going there. In spite of the winter, it must be a delight to live in these mountainous countries. Ah! What a sacred place! Could there be even a trace of sin in such a blessed place! People must be leading a sacred life here, as the sages do.

Slowly, the day came to an end. We left the mountainous terrain to enter the plains. I felt that we had descended on earth from heaven. Dusk set in with sunset. At about nine o' clock in the night we reached Basel, a city situated on the river Rhine, in the north-west of Switzerland. Here again we changed train and it moved at full speed. Everything was dark outside, completely invisible. We only knew that we were crossing Germany through its south-west region. I felt quite tired and went off to sleep after some time.

When I woke up in the middle of the night, I saw that the train had stopped at a station and people were moving about. After sometime an official came to check whether we had anything with us for which we needed to pay a duty. We realised that we had left a country to enter another. Till now we were hearing the harsh German language and now we could hear the sweet soft French. We had entered France. Next morning, we went through the north-west province of France. The land here was extremely fertile; on both sides we could see lush green fields laden with crops. As we reached the plains, the amazing natural beauty that we saw in the past few days were gone. Finally, at one in the afternoon we reached Calais, a city in the north-west province of France.

This city is an important port situated just beside the ocean. From home one could see the vast expanse of the ocean just ahead. Watching the movement of ships and the variety of things being exported or imported, gave one a feeling that, these people are very industrious. The entire city is enclosed by a wall. I have heard that Paris and many other important cities of France are surrounded by walls, just as we find in Delhi, Jaipur and other cities in the north-western part of our country. Calais appears to be a city of ships. There were hundreds of people working in the ships around us— building or repairing them. These gave an idea of how rich and powerful the French are.

On interacting, the French appear quite clever and social. They are famous for their intelligence and technological skills, therefore I need not write much about these people. Many of the French men are quite handsome, and the women are humble and shy. They do not belong to the *babu* class. The poor women work as hard as their husbands do—they till the fields, draw water and help their husbands in many such arduous tasks. Their faces reflect simplicity and a sense of freedom which endeared these French women to me. I have heard that the French mothers are as caring and loving towards their children as our Indian mothers are. They do not neglect their children for the sake of their own pleasure. From their very childhood the French women are given an education and also taught their culture. They develop a fine taste; wear clothes that suit them, and do not spoil their looks by wearing something just for the sake of it. I have heard that they are obedient towards their parents and never marry against their wishes. The French love the outward pomp and show a lot. The churches and other public places are beautifully built, their architectural skills being amazing.

The French are not selfish; the poor, the rich, the middle class, all categories of people sit together to chat and gossip. They are social in nature and interact as friends even with a stranger. The poor people too are extremely modest and I have heard that unlike the poor people of England, they do not behave like beasts after getting drunk. They are quite thrifty, they spend according to their earnings; because of this thrift, they usually do not suffer in drought. The houses in the French cities are made of stones and bricks which reminded me of the houses in Kashi in India. The houses are six to seven floors tall but, the floors are low. I have heard that winters in France are more severe than British winters and the summers are often as hot as in India. After taking our meals at Calais, we boarded a ship at around three in the afternoon. Crossing the Strait of Dover we reached Dover, a city in the south east corner of England at five in the evening. The strait was narrow. Since England and France were quite close to it on either of the banks, water could not flow freely. And then there were violent storms coming from the Atlantic Ocean and the Bay of Biscay. Therefore, there was huge and continuous waves in this strait. Almost everyone suffered here from sea-sickness and threw up. But surprisingly, since the time we started from Bombay and till we reached England I did not suffer from it even for a day.

On reaching Dover, we saw that there was motor vehicle just on the beach, so without any delay we boarded it and started towards London. As I travelled, a new feeling came over me—I, a Bengali lady who had always remained under veil, was in England today. I was in that distant country of England about which I had read and heard so much with such great interest. On twentieth of October, half past eight in the evening, we reached London. We got down at the Charring Cross station. We saw that the station was bright as day time, and all around there were electric lights shining brightly like the sun. Since it was a Sunday, it was not possible to go anywhere else. So we went to quite a big hotel near the station itself. Travelling for twenty four days through water and land had left us extremely tired. Today, after a long time we took complete rest, free from all tension, and in a house which did not move.

REFLECTIONS

A few months have passed since I reached England. I have adopted English ways in matters of food, attire, and other things. Perhaps my fellow countrymen would taunt me as a 'pucca memsahib'. Let them! Their taunt will not affect me anymore. Everybody can make fun of others. In most such cases it is prompted by superstition and lack of experience. This habit of ridiculing found among our fellow countrymen is often the deterrent to our progress. If someone ventures to try something new the entire country joins together to make fun of him. People pounce upon him without even judging the merit of the endeavour, and later when the idea turns out to be good, no one cooperates with him. Rather, they turn away. In every country a new effort is initially ridiculed. But the difference between others and ours is that in our country people are reluctant even if the adopted way proves efficient while in these countries people appreciate such men. Well, those who are incapable of assessing and accepting the inner qualities and virtues of others and imitate only the outward appearance are justly the subject of ridicule. But then it is also important to keep in mind that change in appearance such as clothes etc, does not mean a change of heart, and just by wearing foreign dresses, love for one's own country is not lost. Say, when a person returns from abroad and dresses in a different manner, we must try to understand whether there has been some real progress in him regarding other issues. We must look for any positive change in his mentality as a result of staying in a more developed and independent country and see whether he has imbibed some of the virtues of the foreigners. Suppose we agree that all foreign dresses are bad, but if with such an insignificant aberration the person inculcates genuine virtues—would not that be more worthwhile!

There is no sound logic behind the idea that imitation in any form is wrong. Imitation is of two types, good and bad. People very easily pick up what is bad; especially the superstitions and traditions of the foreigners. That is why the Indians are against imitation in any form, irrespective of its merit. Once, even I was completely against copying, but now I have learnt that without imitating what is good in others, people and country cannot progress. Why are the Europeans so civilized and advanced? A closer look will convince most of you that it has been achieved by the act of imitating.

Whenever they find anything worthy in any other race, they immediately adapt it. Most of the races have similar superstitions. So each race must first closely examine all the other races and discern whether the practices followed by those races are actually better than theirs and if yes, then what makes them so. If we can get proper answers to these two questions and help to inculcate those good attributes within our race, it would be a commendable accomplishment. This is the only way towards progress.

Unfortunately, we are engulfed by superstitions and ignorance. Moreover, the people of our country are so orthodox that it is very difficult to introduce any novelty here; especially, if they see anyone imitating the foreigners in any way, they take leave of their right senses and become hostile towards him. If a person sends his daughter to school till her sixteenth year, people immediately declare him an outcast; if someone's daughter remains unmarried till her fourteenth year, people look for means to ostracize him from the society. It is our misfortune that such incidents are rampant in our country. I know about one of my relatives who did not perform *sashthi puja*[xv]. Consequently, no one attended his son's *annaprashan*[xvi]. For such a trivial shift from the customary ritual more than two thousand people were angry with him and criticized him endlessly. This is a matter of great regret!

The prime reason behind our wretchedness is that we are not aware of our faults and even if we are, we do not try to correct ourselves. It is difficult to find fault with ourselves. Even if we identify those, we do not like to acknowledge them. One who is drowned cannot measure the depth and width of the river. Similarly, we who are submerged in darkness after losing many of our positive qualities along with our independence, cannot judge the ways and degrees by which we are inferior.

People determine what is good or bad by comparing themselves to an ideal, so if we just keep to ourselves and not compare us with any other independent and developed race, we can never know our actual status—our virtues and vices. There cannot be any change in a person's mind if he remains stagnant. People can never leave their vices and embrace the qualities present in other races unless they interact with them. Since, we do not realise our faults and miseries of our life, we remain like inert objects: we do not move in any direction nor do we want to. If we compare our lives to that of any free human being we shall then know the huge gap that exists between these two kinds of lives and how wretched our lives are!

These days many people say that the Indians on their return from England only abuse their own country and hate it. I do not know how much truth there is in this statement, but I hope that there are no such people who hate their motherland. I can say this much that those who come to Europe (obviously those who have brains), learn many things from their stay in this free and civilized country and therefore can better understand the condition of their own country. After coming here they wake up to the reality of their country and feel pained to see the wretched condition there. Perhaps for that reason when they return to their country and point out at the pitiable conditions of India, people misunderstand them and make such false accusations against them.

When we travel abroad we see many new things— new country, new city, new trees, new mountains etc. We derive a lot of pleasure and contentment from those new sights of nature; we are amazed to see huge palaces and buildings; to sum up—we feel really happy to come across a variety of new things. But from where do we get proper education—from all these inanimate things or from man and his nature? If you talk of the beauty of nature—the overwhelming beauty of nature that one gets to see near the Himalayas in our country, cannot be seen anywhere else in this world. And if you talk of the man-made beauties of palaces and buildings, no building can be compared to the temple of Ellora and the Taj Mahal in our country. Then what attracts us more—people or inert objects?

Many countries share similar natural conditions. But in spite of their having such similarities, there are other issues in which they differ completely. Difference between human beings is the chief reason behind it. Of course it goes without saying that any two countries which differ in the weather conditions will have people with different dispositions; but it has been often seen that even in countries with similar climate, people's temperaments differ. This is because people belonging to different countries are different in nature. We also see that in the same country there arise different situations at different points of time. India itself is one such example. The weather condition that we have today is the same as we had in ancient India, but what was the condition of the Indians then and how is it now! I have talked about Italy earlier; in Greece too we can find a similar example.

In the ancient times, like Indians, the Greeks too were famous for their culture and learning. The Romans, after adopting the knowledge and refinement of the Greeks, spread it across entire Europe. With time, the Greeks, like Indians, lost their knowledge, intelligence, and many other human virtues along with their freedom. For centuries they remained in complete darkness being totally subjugated by foreign powers; even the name of Greece was almost lost. Now once again they are regaining their splendour gradually. With independence they are slowly regaining their knowledge and culture. This small country of the Greeks has faced a lot of changes yet it has remained as it was in the ancient times.

All these examples tell us that situation in a country changes with changes in human conditions. Conversations with people increase our curiosity and enrich us; when someone returns from abroad, the first thing people ask him is about the residents of that country. It is interesting to describe a country, but it is more useful and educative to observe people and their characters. Therefore, although in these trips we learn and benefit through these ideas, the most rewarding discussions can only be about the people of that country and their character. So, during any trip or stay abroad it is our important duty to learn about all the aspects of that country.

LONDON

London is a vast city; the biggest in the world. It is about ten miles in length and eight miles in width. London is about four times bigger and eight times more populated than Calcutta. Forty lakh people reside here. One needs to drive continuously for four to five days to take a complete tour of the city but still, one will not be familiar with all its roads. Though London is already a vast city, it is still expanding. Wherever you go, you shall come across hundreds of ongoing constructions which merge the adjacent localities with the city. Even five years back there were green fields around London but now there are innumerable buildings instead. Looking at all these it is difficult to believe that a few years back these places were nothing more than villages.

An Indian once described London in a single phrase as "the city of advertisement"[xvii]. Perhaps his comment was provoked by the abundance of advertisements that he found throughout the city. But apart from advertisements London has many other things as well. At first sight you can call it the "city of shops", "city of theatres", or 'city of wealth", but after staying here for a few days it becomes difficult to decide what kind of a city London primarily is. That is why I could not ascribe any particular epithet to it. Wherever you go you shall see similar rows of grey houses standing close to each other. While on some roads there are houses on both sides, on some others there are shops. In our country we do not have such an arrangement of shops and houses. Perhaps, the total number of houses in Calcutta is far lesser than even the number of shops here. The beautifully decorated shops look splendid at night. Their wares shine brightly under gaslight and appear extremely attractive. I have a feeling that such sights appear very tempting to the poor people but they have to suppress that temptation and return home with heavy heart. It is true that without money no one can be happy in London. It is a treasure house where only the rich can enjoy life.

London is divided into eight parts: north, east, south-west, west, north-west, south-east, central-east and central-west. These divisions have been made by the postal department. In order to write a letter to someone, the house number, the name of the road, and also the part of London in which that road is situated must be mentioned. The north and the north-west divisions are chiefly occupied by middle class people; a few rich and some poor people may also be found there. The house rent is not very high and good accommodations are available at a cheap rate.

Unless explained, people of our country may not understand the concept of 'getting an accommodation'. Here, many people rent a house for themselves and let out a few of the rooms; many families also let out a few rooms of their own house, furnished or unfurnished. Those who offer furnished rooms also provide all the basic services like cooking, making the beds, and cleaning the rooms for the tenants. You will use their belongings, eat in their utensils, and sleep in their bed. If you tell the mistress of the house what you wish to eat each day, she will cook it for you. You only need to pay her the charges for accommodation and food every week. Women who own these houses are known as 'landladies'. The quality of the accommodation depends on the rent paid. If you pay twenty-five shillings per week, which is almost fourteen rupees, you will get two well-furnished rooms on the first floor of a house in an upper class neighbourhood. There will be a comfortable bed, hand and face wash, cupboard for clothes, mirror, pictures etc. The drawing room will be furnished with a table, four or five small chairs with cushions, two sofas, a small couch, a big mirror, pictures etc. Such houses often have carpeted floors. You can get a house at a much cheaper rate as well but either that will not be as good or will be situated in a poorer locality. Unfurnished rooms are also available and they cost even lesser, but then one will need to buy all the furniture and utensils and on top of all these one would also need a maid for all the household chores. Therefore, it is more convenient for the foreigners and newcomers to rent a furnished room. Such furnished rooms are let out not just in London but also in other parts of England as well as throughout Europe. Staying in such a room saves a lot of hard work and time. You can enjoy a sumptuous meal in your house within an hour of returning from a long journey. There are hotels almost everywhere, but they would charge double the amount of what one spends here.

The gentry of London live in the West and Southwest parts of the city. It is difficult to get an accommodation here and even if it is available, it is extremely expensive. If you stand on this side of the road, you can see rows of tidy buildings, standing as tall as mountains on either side. The more you see this place, more you would wish to live there. But all these houses ask for an exorbitant rent of about two to three hundred rupees a month. The main roads in this part of London are better than those in the other parts. The shops here contain a greater variety of commodities which are also more expensive. Looking at the rich people and the expensive items in this place it becomes difficult to believe in the existence of any poor person in London. The palaces of the Queen and the Prince of Wales, Parliament house, royal offices and many great buildings are situated in this part of the city.

All the offices are situated in the central-east and central-west parts of London. In the central-west division there are many theatres, schools, colleges, important offices and shops. The central-eastern part is known as the 'city'. This place reminds me of Burrabazar of Calcutta though it is not as unclean and unhygienic. Here there are banks, huge industries, numerous shops etc. Every building has a shop or a few offices. There are a number of narrow lanes and by lanes here. The houses on either side of the roads are huge and they are so black that they appear to be covered with slime. This place is extremely crowded throughout the day and no one wishes to go out unless required. There is a steady flow of vehicles on this road at all times of the day. The pavements on both the sides are so crowded that one has to move very carefully and slowly, or even stand still at times. Here price of land and house is double than those in our Burrabazar area.

Eastern part of London is starkly different from the rest of the city. Houses here are small and untidy; roads are narrow and dirty, most of them being by lanes. There aren't many shops, and those which are there are full of inferior stuff. This is the place where all the labourers, porters, sweepers and all such working class people live. And there are a number of ship manufacturing industries here. You shall not find a gentleman or a wealthy person in this area. All the lower class people reside here. In this country, the poor constitutes the lower class. While in India as well as in other European countries, such people are quite humble and pay due respect to everyone; in England, and particularly in London, they are almost like animals.

After a visit to this part of the city, no one will believe England to be a civilized country or that there is any gentleman living here. This part of London is vast and has a large number of dingy houses; four or five different families stay together in a small house. Each family has four to five children. One family cannot occupy more than one or two rooms and there are no open courtyards for the children as we have in our country. In one room seven to eight people are herded together like animals. London has its equal share of the rich and the poor. In no other place in the world so many rich and poor people exist together. In this part of London people often engage in bitter fights among themselves and even commit murders. And later in this book I shall describe in details how they behave after getting drunk and in what condition they are then found. The paths here are so narrow, dark and dirty and the smell so repelling that I did not have the courage to walk. I have heard that once a foreigner wanted to meet these people in order to know their condition better, but the guard stopped him from doing so because these people in general were quite beastly by nature and when they got drunk, they completely lost their senses. If any stranger or foreigner went there, that person might face problem.

In London, there are a number of places for sight-seeing, like the Eden Gardens of Calcutta. They are known as 'lungs of London'. Since the city is vast and overcrowded with buildings and people, these parks provide a breathing space. The largest among these is the Regent's Park, situated in the northwest part of London. It is almost three miles wide. There is no pleasure in visiting this place in the winters, the trees are shorn of leaves—the field is full of dry grass – no flowers—on the whole it looks rather dismal. From a distance it appears that a grey field with leafless trees, resembling a crematory, lies ahead.

Yet there is a sort of bliss here as well. On any of the evenings, if you go and sit on one of the benches beside the lakes, you can see flocks of ducks swimming in the lake, flying to and fro their nests. North wind creates ripples in the lake similar to those seen in rivers. In the middle of the water body there is an artificial island of various kinds of plants. They do not look appear attractive. Once here, it would seem that one is in some village, far away from London. There is no clamour from the city here; neither the steady sound of traffic, nor the din of human voices disturbs my ears. Though this is a man-made garden, one can enjoy nature's bliss and forget boisterous London for some time. In spite of chill biting in the limbs, I do not feel like leaving this secluded place.

In summer, Regent's Park looks completely different. The grey trees deck themselves up in new leaves. In between there are the beautiful flower-beds. This country does not have the variety of fragrant flowers as we do, but they take care of what they have and arrange them so beautifully that the flowerbeds look like pieces of painting. All the gardens of London that we have visited reflect the extreme attention and care that the British lavish on them. In our country flowers and fruits grow without much of human endeavour. But in this country, growing even a small plant requires a lot of hard work.

Moreover, in this polluted atmosphere of London, it is not easy to maintain a flowerbed. Wherever I have visited, I have noticed the care and perseverance in all their work. They do not leave any work incomplete, and if they find any flaw, they try to correct it, however difficult it might be. I have seen a few Sanskrit books printed in England; I wonder how they could print them so beautifully and precisely. Since they did not know the language they arranged the types merely by looking at the letters as images. This is a very difficult work which requires a lot of patience. Though printed in this way these books contain very few mistakes. On the other hand, though the Bengali books in our country are printed by Bengalis, most of them have numerous printing errors!

If you visit the park in summers, you will always find people there; that place is really crowded during the holidays.

In this country, flowers bloom only for four months in a year; this is the period when the trees and gardens look beautiful. In just these four months, the British try to enjoy as much as possible. In these gardens, during the three summer months, music programmes are organised thrice a week. Whoever wishes may attend these. There is no discrimination between the local people and foreigners; no vile words are exchanged on account of being 'natives' or 'sahibs'. Everyone can enjoy equally. There is the Eden Garden in Calcutta, built by the British but they do not want the Bengalis to visit and enjoy in that place along with them. During summer, men and women row boats in the Regent's Park Lake as a kind of exercise. There is a place in the park where people play games like cricket, lawn tennis etc. In the central part of the park is a very small botanical garden, created for educational purpose. On the other side is a zoo, which though much smaller than the Alipore zoo in Calcutta, has many animals brought from different countries.

Indians cannot even imagine the dense fog that London experiences. There is fog in other parts of England too but that is not as dense and hazy as it is in London. Fog here is at least four times denser than what we have in the early dawns; say four o' clock in the month of *poush*[xviii]. In November, December and January, fog is densest here. It is caused due to smoke. London has too many motor vehicles. The chimneys of each of the houses emit so much of smoke during winters that at times smoke becomes heavier than the surrounding air. At such times air cannot rise much higher and hangs just over the city. It is this fog that makes the entire city dark. Sometimes such thick fog remains throughout the day and assumes different colours—grey, or black or yellow.

One day I woke up at eight in the morning to find it dark outside; nothing was visible and one had to switch on the lights in order to work. Only those people who had some urgent work could be found on the streets, groping their way through the darkness. No houses or buildings were visible, there were lights in every shop but the fog made the city look very dull. All kinds of vehicles, including the big ones such as trams and omnibuses, were moving slowly. Apprehensive of fatal accidents due to darkness everyone drove at a slow speed. Though generally there are hundreds of motor vehicles on London roads, there was not much noise at that time. In fact there was complete silence all around. The city appeared lifeless. Nothing was visible while walking along the road and one had to walk cautiously. Darkness during the day is worse than that of the night because this darkness caused by fog cannot be removed by any artificial light. Breathing becomes difficult; a kind of black oily substance enters our nose and obstructs the air passage. Lights look dull. I could not work properly as I had to grope in the dark. One becomes depressed, unfocussed and languid in such times. Such times are very trying for people, particularly the foreigners like us. It seems like hell. On such difficult days we wished to run away from London. London loses its charm in such times and the densely populated wealthy city of London turns into a city, shrouded in an odious darkness.

Fog is common in winter, but it remains very dense only for a few days in a year. Had it been an everyday affair, no one could have lived here. On some of the days, the sky is clear for quite some time. Sometimes it is foggy just for an hour or two. Often a clear morning suddenly becomes overcast with dark clouds, and we seem to be plunged in the dark underworld. Windows cannot be kept open when there is fog because the entire room becomes full of smoke. At such times, people go about their work quietly, with their eyes and nose almost shut. They do not laugh, have fun or talk. Everyone use exclamations like, 'what a horrible fog!', 'So difficult!' etc to express their anguish.

Just as there is a prevalence of dense fog in the beginning of the winter, certain years end with an extreme snowfall. But that is not as difficult and intolerable as fog and it is quite nice to watch the snow. There is snowfall throughout England but, it is very heavy in the north. December, January and February are the months for snowfall but at times it happens during March and April as well. The sound of a snow fall is very similar to that of a light drizzle. Slowly, the roads, roofs of the houses, window sills, etc, all turn white. Wow! It feels wonderful! There is no other sound; walking on the road, seems like walking over a layer of flour. There is no sound of footsteps or moving vehicles; London, which is otherwise so noisy, suddenly becomes very quiet.

After snowfall, roads of London become quite dangerous for walking. They become very slippery due to snow on the paved footpath, and therefore at every step there is a chance of falling down. People stay indoor as much as possible, yet none of the work places remain closed. All of them stay busy with their own work. Children enjoy a lot during this period. In spite of the severe cold they play on the roadsides, collecting snow and making snowballs. Indeed, it is a pleasure to see the early morning London dressed in white. Again, if you go to the countryside by train, you can see miles after miles of land covered with snowflakes, turning everything white. There is no grass. And the leaves of the taller trees covered with ice appear like big white feathers hanging from trees. Hailstorms are quite rare here. Due to severity of cold in winter snowfall is a common occurrence.

Though everything in this country was new to us one particular scene appeared quite unique. I have heard that all the foreigners find Sundays in London very unusual. Here is a typical Sunday. People slept till eight or nine in the morning. Many woke up even later. When I woke up I found the city silent. All the fancy shops along the roads were shut. Everything was closed. Peddlers' calls did not pierce our ears; everyone was quiet. The great noise of London could not be heard. It seemed as if everyone had left the city. All recreational centres were closed, there was no fun in strolling on the roads, and everything appeared depressing. Slowly, as the day progressed, one could hear sounds of people around. London was waking up from a long sleep. After a while bells started ringing in all the churches and I came to know that everyone would be visiting these. Sunday is the day of worship for the Christians. All the people, dressed in their finest outfits, go to the church. Both the rich and the poor have special dresses for Sundays, just as we have for our festivals. Women in particular dress up quite elaborately on such days. All women, old and young, get extremely busy with their dresses and the unmarried girls engage in their effort to outshine each other. Everyone comes out in new and bright clothes.

The church bell kept ringing loudly; gradually one could hear the footsteps. Women were in various kinds of dresses. Men did not have much ado about their attire and all of them were in black. Women here, often dress up in the way the *fulbabus*[xix] of our country do while going out. Men do not care much about perfumes or fancy dresses. There were more women on roads than men. I have seen that in every country, women are more engaged in religious activities than men and they are also more conservative. Many women here visit the church just to appear religious while the young girls go there to show off their dresses and to hunt for grooms. Slowly, all of them left their houses banging their doors behind, and only the maidservants stayed back. They did not have any rest even then.

In this country, the church holds prayers thrice a day—at eleven o' clock, three o' clock and seven in the evening. The mode of worshipping is similar to that of our Brahmo Samaj. After working hard for six days, the people take rest on Sunday in keeping with the Bible. The orthodox ones do not work on this day. Many people cook Sunday's food on Saturdays itself. They do not read any book apart from the religious ones; do not sing anything apart from religious songs. I have heard that in Scotland, people do not even read newspapers on this day. There are also people who do not talk about anything apart from religious matters on Sundays.

Many modern Londoners do not observe these so strictly anymore. Most of the people who practice such superstitions are also devout Christians. They actually worship God although they can be seen praying to Christ. There are a few people who go to the church simply to show off, but most of them have go there because they have accepted prayers as the only way to salvation. If someone cannot go to church on a Sunday due to health problems or simply because he loves to pray in solitude, then he can do so at his own house with his wife and children. One can also see here the ailing parent lying on a bed surrounded by daughters who sing melodious hymns and pray for quick recovery of their parent. Is this not a touching scene?

On Sundays, when the weather is pleasant, most people go out in the afternoons and evenings. All major roads are full of people, in some places the poor and servants outnumber others. Gardens are more crowded, as everyone wants to relax on this day of the week. Compared to the rest of the week, on this day people wear cleaner and better clothes. Sundays are holidays for everyone; even the servants are given a break for a few hours in the evening. On main roads, different people move about in such different attires that it becomes difficult to differentiate the gentlemen from the lower classes. Shops, except those selling liquor and tobacco remain closed on Sundays. The liquor shops open for a short period in the morning and remain open throughout the evening. What an amazing race! Of all the shops only the wine shops open on Sundays. In the mornings, people are busy going to churches while the evenings are spent at liquor shops.

People get depressed by a foggy or a rainy Sunday. No one can leave the house or go to the garden to enjoy; everyone has to remain shut indoors. There is neither the bustle of going to church nor the spectacle of women going out in their splendour. Very few people can be seen walking on the roads, carrying their umbrellas. The 'squares', the roads and the gardens are desolate, silent and depressing; looking as terrible as a graveyard. It is beyond my capability to describe such a heart-rending scene but, this occurs quite often in London. It drizzle fast causing slush all around and pools of stagnant water at places. There is incessant rainfall and along with it the smell of smoke and soot everywhere. A rainy Sunday is unbearable by itself, to add to woe, it is accompanied by fog at times. Along both sides of dreary roads, dark houses appear like a heap and dense yellow fog can be seen across the sky. There is no breeze at all. Dirt and soot come down along with the fog. Such a scene is terribly oppressive. On such a day if someone saunters along one of the main roads for an hour the person might even feel suicidal. For us, who have come from the land of clear, bright sky and white mansions, such Sundays in London appear dreadful.

THE BRITISH RACE AND THEIR CHARACTER

Generally the British appear strong, brave, industrious and intelligent. Many among them are more than six feet tall, muscular and robust. Such men are mostly soldiers, peacekeepers, or the bodyguards of high ranking officials. Not only here but throughout the world men of such stature are recruited for the tough jobs of a soldier or a guard. The affluent section of this country also employs such physically impressive men as their chief attendants, perhaps to show off their status.

The master takes every care to see that the attendant maintains his figure and the attendants are equally mindful as well. These attendants look like puppets in their shining brass-buttoned coats, white gloves and tall hats. Dressed in this fashion they stand for the vanity of the rich. Men of such physical stature are found among both commoners and gentry. Their well-built physique, broad chests and long arms make them look like warriors.

In England, I have come across strong and well-built women as well. When these ladies, fashionably dressed, ride past in great speed, they resemble goddess *chamunda*[xx] all set for war. Children here are healthy and good looking. Their fair and young faces remind me of fresh red roses. Village children are healthier and stouter than the urban ones. Their well-developed bodies indicate that they too will grow into healthy adults like their parents. Boys, seven or eight years old, show amazing strength and capacity to work. Though young, they are very enthusiastic. Throughout the world these young men are noted for their bravery and valour; they are healthy and strong, and are fond of physical exercises. They hate to remain idle. They eat healthy and spend their time in wrestling, playing cricket, rowing boats or riding horses. They are adept in all types of physical activities.

From an early age they learn to be brave, patient and capable of enduring hardships. They undertake various heroic feats. The British youth is daring by nature and enthusiastically wait for a chance to meet danger. They are not scared of climbing rugged mountains or swimming at the base of a steep waterfall or hunting in dangerous forests even if there are chances of getting one's head smashed or drown to death

There are people of medium height as well. They are calm and patient. They do not seem to belong to the race described above. They are also very different from other races like Indians, Persians, French, Italians, etc. I have never seen such people earlier. Their faces are expressionless which make them appear lifeless. They have dull, stony eyes. I shall not be exaggerating if I call them heartless because even if they have one, there is no external manifestation of its existence. They never give into anger or any other emotional outbursts for trivial reasons. They seem to move mechanically and are always so quiet and solemn that they seem to be going through a rigorous penance. Gentle emotions such as kindness, generosity, etc are rare among them. They are the ones who remain steady in times of crisis and patient in the face of danger.

There is another type of British people. Their appearances are of various kinds—some are huge and strong, some are quite short and weak; but they are well-known for their courage, enterprise, tolerance, capability to work, etc. They are not easily dissuaded from any task even if they fail at it a hundred times. Earning money is the chief motto of their lives. Their greed for money inspires them to overcome difficulties, take up arduous and life threatening tasks and to willingly go to dangerous places. They are the ones who set up industries or trade in different countries and make their country prosperous.

Everybody in England seems to worship selfishness. They look for their profit always and at all cost. They will never do anything unless it benefits them and once they find any prospect of profit, they will accomplish it at all costs. They believe that all other countries and races of this world exist to fulfill their desires. These British people are like vultures, they not only refuse to share anything with others but also covet what others have. Though they are wealthier than other races, they are always discontented. 'I shall possess everything'; 'I shall own everything'; these are the thoughts that constantly resonate in British hearts. Their limitless greed has driven them to all the corners of this world. And because of this British Empire has gradually expanded and is still expanding.

Money is the supreme god of England. Anybody spending a few days in England will get the hint of how much these Englishmen crave for money and how they pursue it. They earn money both in their own country and abroad. Just as vultures hover around a place where they can smell meat, British rush to any place that has a slightest chance of earning money. Probably there is no such country they are not sucking money from. While making money they do not even care for right or wrong. They do not suffer from any guilt pangs while extorting money from other countries by unfair means. They explore every possible opportunity of earning from India and other countries. They caused immense bloodshed and incurred heavy expenses in order to introduce opium forcefully into China. Such is the stronghold of Mammon in England that even after poisoning the Chinese in this way for their selfish profiteering the British did not suffer from any guilt conscience. In India, China, Germany, France, and other countries, knowledge and wisdom are worshipped more than money, but in England money is supreme. In our country, a poor but educated Brahmin is revered by kings as well and the king does not consider it beneath his dignity to step down from his throne in *galabastra* touch the Brahmin's feet[xxi]. But in this country, however wise or knowledgeable a person might be, people will ignore him and respect someone foolish but wealthy. Wealth being so important here it is not amazing that even the educated will hanker after it.

The British are very proud of their wealth. Sprawling empire and immense wealth have made them excessively arrogant. They consider the entire world to be at their feet and all the other races inferior to them. They firmly believe that they are the first among all the civilized people of the world and better than the rest in terms of knowledge, wisdom and strength. If any race differs from them in any particular aspect, they express their contempt for those people. Countries such as France, Germany, etc are neither less civilized, nor backward in terms of knowledge, wisdom, prowess, or courage when compared to England; rather, in many aspects they are much better than the British.

Yet, the arrogant British express their contempt for the different customs, rites, principles and lifestyle of these people. When they visit other European countries, they behave arrogantly considering themselves superior to the people there. They constantly try to prove that they are better than others. In England, when foreigners talk to them, they maintain a stern look and go around bragging. The common people cannot tolerate the foreigners at all. The British go to different countries to bring back whatever they can. But they are intolerant of foreigners in their own country.

It is not surprising then that these people will look down upon us or consider us uncivil. It is the Indian blood that has nourished the British so far; because of India they can be so arrogant. Such excessive pride comes only before fall. This pride has led to the fall of the Roman Empire. And again it is this pride that caused a prosperous country like France to lose its face in an unfair war against Germany.

The British do not have caste discriminations like the Hindus but they have severe class distinctions. This discrimination is based not on religion but exclusively on money. The Lords never get their wards married to common people nor do the rich come forward to marry the poor for the fear of being ostracized by their society. Caste discrimination in India seems much better when compared to the way the rich people here loathe the poor. In this country, a rich but foolish man considers himself superior enough to insult a wise and level-headed poor person. Here the one who draws a salary of five hundred rupees a month will contemptuously look down upon another who earns only three hundred; a person having ten rupees does not want to speak to another who has eight rupees as he considers himself to be much better than the latter.

This division of class has caused much harm in this country. Common people instead of caring for the poor ones flatter the lords and the other rich men. The wealthy, busy with their selfish motives; are not concerned about the poor. It is because of this contempt of the upper classes that the poor in England do not grow up to be civil and educated in spite of all the available facilities. They do not ever get a chance to interact with the gentry and therefore they do not know what civility is. Just as it is gratifying to meet the educated gentlemen of this country, it is as loathsome and regrettable to meet the uneducated lower class. It is a matter of deep regret that, these people live in a civilized society and yet remain deprived because of the evils of class distinction. It is also abhorrent that these people behave abominably and do not have any self respect or respect for others. In our country we have the rich and the poor but in England, there is the gentleman and the lower class. The social structure in this country makes life difficult for the penniless. Without money one cannot claim to belong to the gentry or interact with them. It is often seen that many poor gentlemen here are ultimately forced to live with the vulgar. After living with them for sometime these gentlemen lose their natural virtues and start behaving like the lower class people. The lower class is the cruellest and worst of all the classes in this country. They behave almost like wild animals.

Tender virtues of love, affection, humility, kindness, charity etc are rarely present in the hearts of the English people. Their heart seems to be as hard as stone. Neither misery, nor happiness of others has any effect on them. They are also never dissuaded from their purpose by mere words. Generally they do not have any empathy even for their next of kin. They torture the weaker ones and do not sympathise with the miserable. They keep quiet in the face of spirit or courage, but do not spare the humble or the cowardly. Like dogs, they run away if someone retaliates but keep on teasing the weaker ones. The two great faults of the British are extravagance and alcoholism. Both rich and poor, spend as much as their earning or even more. When it comes to their alcoholic nature, they have no parallels. I shall tell you in details later about how much they have to suffer because of these two evils.

There are many hypocrites among these people. There is generally a difference between what they think and what they express. Most of the time, their politeness is just a sham. The shopkeepers are not genuine when they sweet talk to charm you; rather, it is money that makes them so polite. The generosity that many of them show towards a foreigner is just a show. Such professional politeness is prevalent among all sections of their society. Foreigners are often taken in by their affectation of hospitality. But after spending some time with them they discover the true nature of their hosts. Though they often indulge in them, they act innocent. The British have all those vices that are generally present in other races, but they never acknowledge it. Though they often indulge in them, they act innocent. Just as they only wipe their lips after eating and consider them to be clean, they think that just by feigning solemnity they can be saintly in spite of the evil in their hearts.

Many Englishmen imitate the mannerisms of the gentry and consider themselves to be true gentlemen. Such people are known as snobs; no one outside the British race can describe the snobs in the way in which Thackeray[xxii] has done. Many foreigners call the British a race of fake believers. Truly I doubt whether any other race overdoes everything as much as the British. Each feigns to be richer than he actually is; many people have to forego meals or pawn their valuables in order to maintain a gentlemanly status. It is difficult to identify the actual class of the people one meets on roads by their attire; but their faces and attitude reveal their knowledge, wisdom and wealth.

For the common people refinement is nothing more than a show; to all intent and purpose they are still as uncultured as before. However, one can still find some civilized people among those who have travelled to other places and interacted with different types of people; but in general, the common people are not really civilized. In spite of all their education and intellect, they are blindly superstitious. This is evident from their interaction with the foreigners. If a person's appearance differ, they stare at him as if they are staring at some beast. Sometimes even the elderly people join the children in making fun of such people and commenting derisively. I have heard from a foreigner that initially when she could not speak proper British English, the shopkeeper, instead of being compassionate laughed at her and made fun of her. One day in a fair I saw a crowd laughing at something. Initially, I had thought that it must be some strange animal or a monkey dance show. But on approaching nearer I found that they were making fun of a Chinese. One woman was waving her hand in front of him and making faces; another was tugging at his plaited hair. That unfortunate Chinese laughed at their barbarism, but they were not at all ashamed. Perhaps no other civilized race indulges in such a shameful act. At least we, the uncultured Indians do not behave in this manner with any of the foreigners.

In fact the British culture is derivative. The Hindus, the Greeks, the Arabs and other races had created their own cultures; but the British—from their beginning to end have imitated other races. If the general population of all the countries are compared then this fact can be easily proved. In almost all the countries, it is the rich and the higher classes that form the cultured section. But the real culture of a country is determined by the knowledge, wisdom and conduct of the poor people. Anyway, one of the greatest merits of the British is that they inculcate only the virtues from other races.

However, they do not easily acknowledge that these virtues exist in those races. Once they recognise anything good, they immediately imbibe it. If a person tries something new, rest of them first make fun of him, then keep quiet, and later when they find it to be useful, the entire race accepts it. This is how the British has progressed. We do not imitate anything good from others either out of diffidence or out of fear of being ridiculed; and this is what has brought us so low. There is a story about this British habit of imitating. Previously, they did not use umbrellas; even if it rained hard, they walked on roads getting drenched. Gradually when a few British started using umbrellas following the examples of the French and others, rest of the race started teasing them, calling them French. But in spite of all the mockery those Englishmen did not give up the practice. Later rest of England followed them and learnt to use umbrellas during the rains. Till now, in England, only the children, the aged and the women use umbrella under scorching sun.

In certain aspects, the British are very different not just from us but from other European races as well. In one particular matter however, they are just incomparable; I have not heard or read anything similar among other races. In all the countries, whenever people meet each other on way or at market places or anywhere else, they talk, smile or share a joke and laugh with each other. But the British do not like talking to others unless they are relatives or acquaintances. At crowded places such as roads, railway stations etc, one can hear a deafening roar of vehicles but not any human voices— everyone is quiet and mechanical. Unless introduced by any friend or family member, no one likes talking to or interacting with each other; associating with strangers is against their code of civility.

It is said that a man had once fallen in a hole and cried aloud for help. Just then another British was passing by. On hearing that unfortunate person's cry for help, he said to himself— "Oh, such a bad luck! Had I known that person I could have saved him right now." I do not know whether this story is authentic but their insensitivity often surprises me. I have also seen about ten to twelve people sitting quietly face to face in a train or a tram car. No one will make the first attempt to talk as if it would hurt his ego. I feel an uncontrollable urge to laugh at their habit of remaining mute found among both the gentlemen and the uncultured ones.

Many people say that conversation is like salt in human life; truly, life appears dull without it. I do not understand how the British can be happy without talking to each other. If you enquire about something from a person, he would reply in monosyllable. It appears as if they want to save words more than money. One day, I came across a man thrice, and each time he just said 'it's a pleasant day today'. When the British boys play cricket or football, they try to avoid talking. Even when they are hit by the ball, they express their pain in vague terms. I think that it is because of such horrible climate that the British love to keep quiet. Truly, such is the weather of this place that even mere interaction with the people one meets along the way becomes a difficult task. This silence also signifies certain merits that these British have. They do not talk while at work and concentrate on the task only. They do not lose their presence of mind easily. Even when in deep trouble, they try to find a solution without losing their cool. There are many historical evidences of how the British soldiers maintained their calm during wars and fought with patience in keeping with the rules and regulations.

Till now I was describing the faults of the British; now I shall discuss their virtues. In spite of many vices, their race has an excellent foundation. Qualities such as efficiency, capacity to work hard, perseverance, spirit, courage, etc have made them civilized and prosperous. It is due to our own faults that we Indians are being dominated by the British and it is due to our incapability that the British are self-interestedly ruling over our country. Most of the British people leave their virtues at home before setting out for other countries. Self-interest is their prime goal, therefore in foreign lands, their selfish propensities become stronger. Particularly, when they are in their colonies, their nature undergoes a drastic change. Thus, we consider all the British people bad as we get to see only the darker side of their nature in India.

Since we have been under foreign rule for a long time, we are not always capable of appreciating the virtues of a race which is free. It is not right to overlook their virtues and discuss their vices only. The British people have achieved such greatness only because of their merits. If the British had nothing but vices then we would not have known about them at all and I too would not be writing this book.

For the British, work is like their constant companion. They love to work; the reason could either be weather or their natural propensity. They do not shy away from hard work nor do they tire easily. But in our country, perhaps due to the weather or sheer indolence, people grow weary just after working for a couple of hours. A British is not tired after five or six hours of work and do not require rest at short intervals. If you observe them while they are at work such as constructing roads or buildings you will realise that they work with the same spirit and intensity from the first to the last working hour. They are not just efficient but are committed to their work as well. They do not like to waste their own time nor of the others by indulging in unnecessary conversations. They do not wish to pester or be pestered by others. For these reasons, it's a pleasure to work with them.

The British are unparalleled in today's trade and commerce because they are industrious. Trade is their great strength; it is through trade that they have become so prosperous and gained colonies throughout the world. I shall deal with this topic exclusively in a separate chapter. Enthusiasm is another of their merits. They are always on the alert and the moment they find a chance for any new enterprise or trade they pursue it zealously. They constantly invent new machinery, and advance in the fields of industries and handicrafts. They keep a track of all the new inventions and industrial developments taking place in other countries. They try to make those available in their own country too. I have already said, the British are not inferior to any other race in terms of courage and valour. From their first step in life till the end they work with courage. Each chapter of British history speaks of their courage and spirit.

The British are selfish no doubt, but they are also self-dependent and have self-respect. They would be the last one to ask for help if they can accomplish it on their own. They neither help others nor seek other's help. When approached for some help their advice generally is, 'self help is the best help'. Here each person, whether grown up or young, takes care of his own self. In India even the grownup wards find nothing to be ashamed of in remaining financially dependent on their father but not so in Britain. Here such cowardice or indolence is not seen. Once the sons become adults, they seek their own means of earning a living. Even daughters find it demeaning to live idly in their parents' house or be dependent on any of the relatives. Self-reliance comes quite early to them. I have often seen that if a child falls down on the road, he doesn't look at his mother for help. Rather he tries to get up on his own. When he succeeds, his friends, who are themselves very young, and his parents, praise him. If the people of our country had such awareness of self-dependence and self-esteem then the habits of laziness and dependence could never have existed.

One can see great unity among the British. Though they are selfish, their unity has helped them to successfully establish many large industries, business and trade. Without this unity their entire empire and business would have collapsed in a moment. Unity has helped the inhabitants of this small island to achieve so much and without it, we the people of a larger country are unable to accomplish any great task. In this world, there are many tasks that cannot be accomplished singlehandedly, it is not possible for an individual to take a country forward or conquer countries all by himself. It is easy to break a single twig but not a bunch of those. Unity adds to the beauty of a race but, we are completely deprived of that beauty. The British can run a laundry shop or an empire with equal ease only because they are unified. But we are not united anywhere—neither in family, nor in society or country.

The British are not only united but also have a strong love for their race. They are extremely devoted; they cannot put up with any insult to any of their countrymen or bear any wrong done to their country. Just as they are eager to maintain their self respect, they are equally keen to preserve the honour of their race. They are proud of their independence as a race and country. This sentiment does not allow them ever to act wrongly towards their country or their people. If a countryman is tortured, they take that as an insult and try their best to avenge it. If any foreigner beats up an Englishman on the road then fifty other Englishmen would gather there and prepare to beat him up. We do not have such love or devotion towards our own country. Forget about working for the country's upliftment, we are not even bothered if the entire nation goes down the drain. To talk about our love for our own race—if we see a foreigner beating up any of our fellow countryman, we leave that place thinking, 'why should I be bothered if he is being beaten?'

When the British go abroad, they prefer staying together with their own people rather than staying with the foreigners; they help each other and trust their own people more than those belonging to other races. They would never recruit any foreigner for a job if there are Englishmen available and always prefer one of their own people over a better qualified foreigner. Otherwise, they believe, it would be a dishonour to their community. They generally do not indulge in knavery, deceit or falsehood among themselves. They might cheat people belonging to other races but they will never do so to their own. The kind of malice and envy that is seen among the Indians is not generally found in them. The British never ridicule their own race nor do they stoop before anyone.

In this context, I shall briefly discuss another merit of the British. One can find a great sense of duty among these people. Here, right from the prime minister to a minor labourer, each one performs his own job meticulously. Both a high ranking government official and an employee at a very junior level do their work with the same concentration. If you call a carpenter for a job, he will complete the assignment appropriately even without your instructions.

There is no need to monitor his work so as to get it finished in stipulated time. I have often been amazed by their sense of duty. Even in storm, rain or snow, the British people never neglect their duties. Again, just as they themselves do not talk much, they do not waste our time asking for much explanation. The moment they get a job, they get busy with it. They hate abuses or rebuke; and young or old, no one likes to be rebuked or does anything to deserve so.

The British love to travel in foreign countries. Many of them go on a tour of other countries whenever they can manage some time. They visit France, Germany, Italy, Spain,

America, and often go up to India or Australia. In this way, they come to know about the conditions of the different countries and their people. Many of them save money throughout the year to visit foreign countries during their holidays. After going there, they gather information regarding those people and also learn their language in order to understand them better.

Not just men but even women undertake these trips along with their husband, father or brothers. There are very few gentlemen here whose sons have not travelled to other countries of Europe. The British regard travelling to foreign countries as a part of their education therefore, most of the rich people here consider it their duty to visit other countries with their families, as and when possible. Travelling helps in eradicating superstitions; new sights make them wiser, new feelings help to develop their minds and living with unfamiliar people help in their self-development.

Though the British are not at all affectionate towards foreigners, they also do not disturb them without a cause. Many people from other countries have taken shelter here after being tortured in their own over religious or other matters. Though the British do not like these people, they do not make lives difficult for them and at times even show them some generosity. Just as there are extremely selfish people in this country, I have seen some humble and noble people as well. Many rich men of this country are always engaged in charitable works and donate huge amount of wealth for the benefit of the others.

Several British men are world famous for their charity; they always donate large sums of money for various purposes within their country and also send huge amount during crisis in other countries. The British are neither obsessively polite nor extremely rude. Though they are hard at heart, they are rarely mean minded. It is difficult to forge a friendship with the British but, if you once become friends, then it is hard to find a more helping, loyal, and enduring friendship. Most of the educated British are polite. After interacting with them, we feel respectful towards them and tend to forget all the flaws of their race. They are the chief assets of England who bring glory to their country.

QUEEN VICTORIA AND HER FAMILY[xxiii]

Every Indian must be curious about the one who has sovereignty over our country and who, with the help of the parliament, is ruling over the entire kingdom of England in perfect law and order. Empress Victoria is not indisposed towards India; she tries her best for the happiness and well-being of the Indians. But we are not a free country. Today the sceptre of Hindustan is in the hands of the British, instead of the Hindus. It is not the Queen's fault that the crown of India today shines brightly on her forehead. Since we are under her rule, our benefactress should try her best towards our welfare.

The queen was born in the year 1819. She was coroneted at the age of eighteen. At twenty-one she was married to the German prince, Prince Albert. Now she is sixty-five years old and she has been ruling the country for forty-seven years. Her skill in running the government even in this old age is amazing. In her kingdom neither the guilty is let scot-free nor is the innocent punished. The queen herself has set example that moral transgression should be universally hated and treated as a heinous sin. She is a true *sati*; no blemish has ever touched her character. She has all the qualities of compassion, charity, etc. She is unparalleled in the feminine virtues such as love and affection. Through her years of just rule she has proved herself capable of running a government.

Prince Albert, Queen's husband expired in 1861. She was almost mad with grief. Since then she does not like meeting too many people or making public appearances. She spends most of her time in solitude in the mountainous regions of Northern Scotland. A statue of Prince Albert named 'Albert Memorial' has been erected in the Kensington garden in London to offer her some contentment. Her husband was also as honest and virtuous as she. He had a great love for literature, science and art. England had made great progress in these fields under his care and it was due to him again that the Great Exhibition was first organised here.

Queen Victoria is herself very religious and expects the others to be so too. If the moral disposition of any of her grooms or maids arouses her suspicion, she immediately expels the person from her palace. She also tries her best to help her servants lead an honest life. I have heard that her eldest son, the Prince of Wales, was a philanderer in his youth. There were a lot of rumours about him. In consequence, for many years the Queen refused to even see him though he was her own son. Later, when the prince fell very ill and begged for her forgiveness, the mother within her relented. She paid him a visit and once again talked to him. Since then the prince has taken a vow to mend his ways. Such an exemplary deed has touched everyone's heart. Everyone is grateful to her for her impartial judgment and rule; everybody is happy with her.

The queen now has three sons and four daughters. She had four sons and five daughters but unfortunately a few years back she lost her second daughter Princess Alice. These losses, that of her husband and her daughter gravely affected her. Then again, some days back, she received another rude shock in the form of death of her youngest son, Prince Leopold, Duke of Albany. The prince was very kind and scholarly. Not just the queen but all the people of England were heart-broken for him.

Unfortunately, he had married just two years back. Everyone was also sympathetic towards the young widow, the Duchess of Albany, who had to accept such a fate at such a young age. In spite of such grave tragedies, the Empress still manages her affairs of the state with a remarkable fortitude. This has earned her commendations from one and all. It is rare to find such a religious and virtuous woman in such a prosperous country. I hope she would become an example for every Indian woman.

For the most part of the year, the Empress lives at the Balmorals Castle in Northern Scotland. She spends a couple of months in a small island named Wight in the south of England and then spends about three months in the city of Windsor, about twenty miles from London. She does not like to stay in London, and if at all she has to stay here, then she stays at Buckingham Palace. If any foreign king, queen or prince comes to London, the heir to the throne, the Prince of Wales welcomes them on behalf of the queen.

It needs no mention that the Empress has a large household. In her household there are at least a thousand office-bearers, servants, maids etc. Among them many hold hereditary posts. All of them receive a generous wage; some of them are quite handsomely paid. The chief of her staff is called the 'Lord Steward'. He has to look after the entire household. Only those who work in the Queen's bedchamber, her stable and the Chapel Royal are exempted from his authority. The rest of the staff obeys his orders and execute them promptly. He can bring them to book for any kind of misdeed and resolve their quarrels. But all his actual tasks are in fact done by another employee. The Lord Steward has to be present in the court during all its proceedings. His salary is two thousand rupees a month.

The person under Lord Steward is the 'Lord Treasurer'. In the absence of the former, he has to be there during all the activities of the state. His salary is nine hundred rupees a month. There is another such official called the 'controller'. He does not have as much work but earns a similar salary. There is another officer called 'The Master of the Household' whose salary is about twelve hundred rupees a month. He is the actual representative of the Lord Steward carrying out the actual duties of the latter and it is he who takes charge of the servants of the palace. There are a number of officials and servants under him who maintain record of the accounts. All these four officials under the Lord Steward can dine with the Queen.

Next in line is the clerk of the kitchen. His salary is seven hundred rupees a month. There are three employees to assist him. They keep the account, weigh all the things purchased and give orders to the shopkeepers. The chief cook of the kitchen also gets a salary of seven hundred rupees a month. He has ten cooks and twelve servants under him who do all the jobs related to cooking. Apart from these, there are fifteen people employed to prepare the desserts and condiments. The chief butler of the palace, or the supervisor of alcohol, earns five hundred rupees a month. He has to select and buy drinks for the royal family and take care of those. He also makes the drink for the Queen and sends it to her. He has five or six subordinates who help in laying the table. It is their job to see that the table is properly arranged before the Empress comes for her dinner.

Ten to twelve people take care of the utensils of the queen. Though they do not have much work to do, their high salary is justified as they are in charge of a number of very precious items. Just Windsor Palace itself has gold and silver utensils worth more than three crores. There are almost thirteen people recruited in the palace just to buy coal. Apart from these there are gate-keepers, doormen, grooms to light the lamps and for various other purposes. The other department of the royal household is the department of Lord Chamberlain. The Lord Chamberlain has to undertake many great tasks. His main duty consists of supervising the servants, maids and keeper of the wardrobe of the Queen's room—to move beddings, furniture, tents etc as and when required, and to oversee the musicians, hunters, various artists, ambassadors, doctors, priests and others. During coronation ceremonies, royal weddings and feasts, he has to look after the entire proceedings. His monthly salary is two thousand rupees. The Treasurer of the Queen is another high official in this department. He too receives a monthly salary of rupees two thousand. He keeps an account of the Queen's money.

There is a man and a woman to look after the Queen's wardrobe[xxiv]. The former earns a salary of eight hundred while the latter gets five hundred rupees a month. Apart from them there are her messengers, mistresses of bedchamber and many other servants. They have a number of women subordinate to them to do the actual chores of the bedroom. There are a number of waiting women as well whose primary job is to help with the Queen's attire. They get a salary of hundred rupees a month each. Apart from these there are so many other kinds of officials, servants and maids that it is almost impossible to describe them all here. There is a royal chapel here for the Queen to pray. The priests and other officials of this chapel are considered to be a part of the royal household. There is a royal orchestra which plays during the coronation ceremony, weddings of the princes and princesses and other occasions. To maintain this orchestra, one has to spend a thousand and nine hundred rupees a month. There is a poet in the royal household called the 'Poet Laureate'. Though his salary is not even a seventh part of the master cook of the Queen, his post is one of great prestige. The present poet laureate is Lord Tennyson. He is the chief poet of England at present. Recently, he has been bestowed with the title of Lord.

The Queen had a very loyal servant by the name of John Brown. He has recently passed away. He was her favourite and most trusted. There was no such place which the Queen visited without him. In one of her books, the Queen has praised this servant a number of times and the death of this old and trusted servant has greatly affected her.

A TOUR OF LONDON

When an Indian steps out on the roads of London for the first time, he might get confused and keep standing like an imbecile. Everything appears different here. Houses, vehicles, people, their dresses, way of talking, etc. are so unlike our country. If you go to any of the main roads, you can see blocks of black, four to five-storied buildings on its either side with nothing but lanes separating them. As far as you go, you will get to see endless roads and buildings. You can see a number of chimneys on every roof, some of them emitting smoke. There is no one upon the slanting roofs, covered with black slate. At some other places you will find wires of different types running over the rooftops. These are wires for telegraph, telephone, etc.

If you look below, there are alluring shops on both sides of the road. Since the shops have a glass front, various items that are kept on display within the shops are visible from outside. Shopkeeper's name and type of the shop are engraved in bold letters on well polished brass or wooden plates, and fixed at the top and bottom of the wall. The roads are very clean and paved with hard stones.

On its either side there are pavements for pedestrians. Hundreds of people belonging to various situations and countries can be seen to be walking together. Very little conversation can be heard but at times you can also hear some foreign tongues. There is an incessant flow of various types of vehicles moving along the roads—brougham, barouche, phaeton, cab, omnibus, shopkeepers' carts, etc. Crossing these roads is quite risky; one has to cautiously look towards both the sides and then cross carefully. There are no palanquins or bullock carts in this country; noise from vehicles drowns human voices on roads. People are fair complexioned and mostly dressed in black. They dress to the best of their ability. You cannot see their bare hands or feet.

There are some roads where traffic is much less. All the peddlers gather there, carrying their merchandise in baskets or hand pulled carts and go up and down the roads calling out loudly. They do not stop to take rest and rend the sky with their shouting. They keep on peddling from eight o'clock in the morning till afternoon and at times even till eight or nine in the evening. Initially, we could not make any sense of their shouting; we could only see their fares.

After a few months I could gradually figure out their words. At times they sell fish in hand drawn carts and call out 'mackerel'. Some peddlers are tin smiths, some call to sharpen knives and scissors and some sell coal. There are a few Jews who call aloud to buy old clothes. On certain roads in the evenings peddlers sell hot roasted potatoes which appear quite tempting in this cold weather. In this way people here shout on top of their voices to sell their merchandise. From six in the morning till five in the evening the milkman pulls his milk cart to deliver milk at every doorstep, shouting 'milk—milko—ko—ku', etc.

At times, we can see a few well-built Irish women carrying milk cans upon their head. But, unlike in our country, this is not usual here. Almost all the vendors own horse carts or hand-drawn carts to carry their commodities. On some evenings a man can be seen walking along certain streets carrying a box on his head. He rings a bell as he walks. And in this way, instead of shouting, he informs everyone that he is selling muffins which is a condiment resembling our own *pitha*[xxv]. At some other place one can see an old woman carrying a small basket upon her head or along her waist and calling out 'watercress'. She sells a kind of leaves which are eaten raw.

Apart from the 'cries' that I have discussed here, there are many other kinds as well. But it is the cries of the newspaper boys that draw my attention the most. They call out 'newspapers' from seven o'clock till eleven in the morning in all the main roads, important crossings and in front of the railway stations. They approach the passersby and ask—"O sir! Which one would you like—the Daily News or the Daily Telegraph?" or "Which newspaper do you need sir, Standard or Chronicle?" In the evenings too, along the crowded areas like the main roads and crossings, these young boys call out the names of the evening dailies like 'Echo', 'Globe', 'Standard', 'Special', etc.

There is no dearth of either newspapers or readers. Since they come quite cheap everyone can afford them. In almost all the roads you can hear 'organ', a kind of a musical instrument, playing a plaintive tune. Many poor Italians come to this country and they play these instruments, walking down the roads. People at times give them a penny or two for their music or out of pity for their miserable condition. Sometimes these musicians also ask for money from people by touching their hats or through other gestures. Since begging is not legal in this country, beggars use various ploys to extort money. If you enter any of the lanes to get rid of the loud noise of the main roads, your ears will be deafened by the jangling sound of the organs played by those poor Italians.

London has numerous shops. They are so well-decorated that people are attracted towards them at the very first sight. Many people have described London as a 'jungle of shops'. I think this name befits the place. Almost everything is available in this great metropolitan city. If you have money you will get everything and within every possible range. I have even seen mangoes here which they import from America. Those which cost only half a paisa in our country are sold here for ten to twelve *annas*[xxvi].

The very fact that it is available here is amazing. It is difficult to get coconuts in the north-western parts of India, but here almost every fruit shop has loads of coconuts. Even in cases of clothes, jewellery or toys, such a huge range of products in terms of variety and price cannot be found anywhere else. Here there aren't any bazaars as we see in our country, but every locality has shops where all the things are available. One has to just go and buy whatever is required.

I have already mentioned earlier that the part of London which is known as the 'city' is full of huge shops. There are important streets like the Oxford Street, Regents Street, Strand Road, etc. which also have a number of big and famous shops full of precious items. London has a number of long roads but none is bigger or grander than the Oxford

Street. Regents Street is very well constructed and the shops along it are brighter as well but, Oxford Street has a greater variety of shops and the shops here are better stocked. And, since this is an old street, there are both old and new types of houses along its sides. Though the Oxford Street is quite big, there is not much space left. House rent here is one hundred and fifty rupees yet none of them remain unoccupied.

Just across the footpath there are four to five storied buildings, some are even six to seven storey high. Each building has a shop and the things are stored in the store-rooms in the floors above. A walk down the Oxford Street gives an idea of England's wealth and grandeur. It has all kinds of shops—jewellery, garments, furniture, glass wares, books, food items etc. All the things that a person might need are available here. Alongside these shops there are also shops selling that ruinous substance—alcohol. They fiercely compete with other shops.

At some places you come across scenes such as the one I am going to describe now: a rich lady, expensively dressed, gets out of her carriage and enters jewellers shop. Immediately four to five young women employees hover around her asking her, 'what do you want ma'am?' and show her the things she wishes to. After some time that lady leaves the place in her carriage. Young boys and girls are dazed by her beautiful carriage, horses, the well dressed coachman and her servants. Elsewhere you can see the tired workers in tattered clothes visiting the liquor shops after their day's work. Some are sitting inside the shop and drinking and some are coming out after finishing their drink. One feels pity looking at them.

There is no dearth of the variety of people walking on the footpath. The daily crowd is similar to the crowd that we have during our festivals or fairs. People walk, stop for a while and again start walking; some of them stand near the glass panes of the shops and ponder what they might buy; some talk to their friends, some of them stand and watch others' dresses and still others stand and gape at the passersby. There are policemen at various points along the roads. They control crowd or stop vehicles near the crossings to help pedestrians cross the roads. Many people can be seen entering and coming out of the shops. All these shops are so fascinating and have such a variety of things that it becomes difficult to make up one's mind. Such is their allure that it is difficult taking one's money back home.

After walking past these shops you will see some old houses being replaced by new buildings. In our country, some Muslim women can be seen working among the masons but here women are not involved in such heavy hazardous jobs. The workers are young men and they work like the busy bees. They have erected scaffolds on each side. These scaffolds are not like those of bamboo that we see in our country; instead they have used strong wooden pillars and planks. I am sure they will laugh at the idea of climbing the bamboo scaffolds which are used in India and if they are asked to do so, they will say that "our lives are not so cheap that we shall foolishly lose it by climbing on such scaffolds". Yet, hundreds of poor Indians climb on these bamboo scaffolds even while constructing huge buildings. Money begets luxury which in turn leads to foppery. Since England is a prosperous country, the British seek their own comfort in everything they do.

The place where these new houses are coming up has been barricaded by wooden planks to stop traffic movement through that area and also to ensure the safety of the pedestrians. These planks look like the walls of a house with multi-coloured drawings on it, similar to those seen in pictures. But on approaching nearer, you will find that it is actually covered with hundreds of advertisement bills— advertisements of a theatre with images of the leading actors, or of some 'music hall' with a picture of a clown, etc.

Someone has invented a medicine for long and black hair. An advertisement shows the efficacy of its product by portraying a woman sitting with her long, flowing hair. There are advertisements of different types of alcoholic drinks with pictures of bottles of different types. Some advertisements present newly published books with the names of the books written in such huge fonts that a man can pass through each letter.

There are innumerable posters and advertisements, and I am not sure whether anyone even reads them. They are just there. Companies use advertisements for their publicity irrespective of any profit from these. Often these advertisements run through such long stretches that they hurt the eyes if anyone tries to read them. The British are crazy about advertising. There is no such place where hoardings are not visible. These are present everywhere—on roads, on the walls of the houses, inside and outside the vehicles etc. At times, hoardings on wooden planks can be seen hanging from people's back as well. In the omnibuses and tramcars one can see advertisements such as "such and such salt is excellent" or "such and such match box is the best". All the walls of the railway stations are covered with such advertisements. It becomes difficult to identify the station's name out of so many brand names in the advertisements. When the train stops at a station, one has to carefully look for its name. And after a long search one might think that the name of the station is 'such and such mustard'. If the person then asks someone whether 'such and such mustard' is the name of the station, the one questioned would burst out laughing. Only then one realizes that the said name is an advertisement of some brand of mustard and not the name of the station. Most of the newspapers here have become rich due to these advertisements. You will see that half or more than half of space in any newspaper that you read is taken up by advertisements. I do not know whether this is for the better or for worse. Any newly published book contains at least twenty pages of advertisements. Advertisements here are costlier than in our country, yet there is no dearth of them. The bigger companies and shopkeepers consider this to be one of their essential expenses. What more shall I say; such profusion of advertisements make the British appear quite stupid at first, but they are hardly wrong in matters of money. They put up advertisements wherever they find some place because they want to maximize profit by minimum investment. I have heard that many companies spend about a lakh on these every year. Often these advertisements help sell trivial objects and raise the profit of the company.

One has to go to 'Hyde Park' via Oxford Street. This garden is situated to the west of London. Though I am referring to it as a garden, it has no fruit trees and very few flower bearing plants. It has a lawn and some big trees at places. It is smaller than Regent's park but if you also include the 'Kensington Garden', a garden full of flowers situated to its south west, then their combined area becomes much bigger than the Regent's park. This appears to have been constructed only for the rich Londoners. Though the poor are not barred entry here, it is surrounded by houses of the rich on all sides and mostly the gentry visit this place. This is so beautifully maintained that no trace of poverty is visible here. There is a big lake within Hyde Park where many men and women go for boating during summers. The rich people come here for a drive in the fresh air and many men and women come here to ride as well. I felt extremely happy to see men and women taking walks together, rowing boats or riding but at the same time felt sad to realise that such a scene is not to be found in my country.

London has most of its visitors between the end of spring and the middle of summer. This is the period when the affluent come to the city to stay. All the lords, including the prince also come here during this time and the parliament is also in session. People from different countries enjoy visiting this place at this time of the year. So for these few months London becomes a bustling city. A visit to the Hyde Park during this time will give you an idea regarding London's wealth and opulence. If anyone from my country visits London, the person should not go back without visiting the 'Rotten Row' in Hyde Park because it has no parallel.

There is an area in Hyde Park exclusively maintained for horse riding. This is named Rotten Row. On a summer day if someone visits this place before two in the afternoon, he would see hundreds of men and women riding horses as a part of their morning exercise. The women outnumber men here. The place becomes so crowded that it appears as if all the well-off folks of London have gathered there. Dense smog hangs over London most of the time and the trees lose their beauty.

But now, dressed in new leaves they provide shelter from the scorching heat of the July sun. On one side of the footpath there is an iron railing and on the other there are beautiful flowers beds and greenery of creeper and foliage. Flowers are all in bloom and their fragrance is carried far and wide by the mild breeze. The breeze would often carry to you the strong fragrance of a rose or some other British flower. We cannot decide whether to praise the gardener or nature for such beautiful and vast flower beds. Tens of thousands of people stand along the sides to admire these. Horse riders, variously attired, gallop past them. The entire scene is as amazing and exquisite as that of a scene from any theatre.

Here you can find people from almost all the races. Almost every civilized country like France, Italy, Germany, Spain, etc has its ambassador here. They ride beautiful horses. At times you can also see a Hindu or a Japanese young man. Here you can find members of the parliament, wealthy businessmen, and aristocrats strolling together in this park.

You can also see women of various age, social position and status. Some of them are highly educated, even graduates, while some are uneducated; some of them are extremely beautiful, while a few are ugly though extravagantly dressed. You will find some chaste women as well as a few of questionable reputation. Nowhere else in this world can you find such diversity of dresses as you can see here. It is difficult to guess the amount of money, skill and different types of materials that go into the making of these dresses. Men and women on horses sometimes gallop fast and at times they take a leisurely ride. Often if they come across their friends, they ride together deep in conversation. After spending their time till two in the afternoon here, they go back to their homes.

I have told you earlier that there is another garden called Kensington Garden adjacent to the Hyde Park which appears to be a part of the latter. Most part of Hyde Park is covered with lawn while there are many big trees in Kensington Garden. This garden looks especially beautiful in summer. Wherever you look there are climbers, plants and many kinds of beautiful flowers. At places there are cool and pleasant bowers surrounded by huge trees. There is a round pond ahead of these which reminds me of the pleasant gardens in the north of our country. But, a big difference is that while in our country every garden has fruit-bearing trees, here they have grass, flowers, flower beds and tall trees.

In this Kensington Garden, there is a huge statue of Queen Victoria's late husband, Prince Albert, built in his memory and named the Albert Memorial. This is one of the important tourist sites here. The metal statue is placed under a beautifully painted and decorated stone canopy. The walls of the canopy have carved images of various great European poets, musicians, sculptors, scholars, scientists, etc. In its four corners, there are four big stone carvings symbolizing the four continents of Asia, Europe, Africa and America. One of the carvings consists of a veiled Indian woman sitting on an elephant and a Chinese and a Muslim standing on her either side.

This represents Asia. In the same way the carving depicting Europe shows a European riding upon a horse; in the African carving, there is an African riding a camel and in the carving for America, an American is sitting on a cow. Looking at these carvings, one can know about the various kinds of dresses that were earlier worn by the people of these four continents. The clothes of the people of Asia and Africa are still very much the same but that of Europe and America has undergone a lot of changes. Previously, the Europeans had turbans on their heads, wooden shoes, and wore dresses like ours, but now they have changed much. Along with their way of dressing, huge changes can be seen in their knowledge too.

It is pleasing to see the images of so many great Europeans carved on the canopy walls. Believing in *Kirtijasya se jeevati* or people live through their deed; I recalled the great deeds of these people and disregarded all other thoughts. Years have passed, yet their names remain inscribed in the hearts of all the civilised and educated people! Look at Shakespeare here holding a book and deep in his thoughts; and here is blind Homer with lyre in his hands, as if he is about to sing right away. Each of these carvings represents the art for which each one was famous and that made these images appear life-like.

London has many wonders but the most amazing one is the London underground. One can see a London above the ground. There is another underneath which is equally vibrant. This is already a big city with its numerous houses. Our country men will be surprised if they know that there are still more houses underground. They might even think these to be very dark and scary. Here the houses on each side of the road have a basement. The rooms in this floor are mostly used as kitchen, laundry, and coal storage. Most of the households use this space for comparatively messy chores like cooking and washing. They use the basement for all those chores which might make the place untidy. Here they store their coal and food stuff as well. Poor people often sleep here. Since there is some empty space in the front and there are windows in these rooms, they get enough light and air. Even these rooms are much cleaner than the kitchens above the ground in our country.

London has a system of underground railways. It continuously goes around London moving under roads and houses. No other country has such astonishing railways. While coming to England, our train did pass through a number of very long tunnels but the experience of moving under the earth in darkness like insects appeared quite new to me. There is no pleasure in boarding these trains. We have to travel through dark tunnels throughout. At times a part of the sky is seen. The stations have dim lighting. They have developed various means to let out smoke and let in fresh air. Even then after travelling for a while, we find the smoke suffocating us, making life difficult. But with time we get used to everything. Thousands of people commute from one part of London to another by these trains. These trains are faster and cheaper modes of travelling as compared to horse carriages for commuting across city. Since the stations are underground, one has to climb down the stairs to board the trains. The stations are quite near to each other—within two miles there are two to three of them. At first it baffles us that while there are so many people, cars, etc moving above the ground, there are also underground trains travelling in darkness. But men, women and children here are quite comfortable commuting in this way.

Apart from this railway, there are various pipelines running underground—such as pipeline for gas, for water, drainage, sewerage, etc. So one can say that London is completely hollow from within. Many a times while walking on the roads, it seems that one is walking on a bridge.

Many people have heard about the tunnel under the river Thames. This is even more spectacular than the underground railway. Previously, it was used for the pedestrians and now it is in use by the railways. I had read in my childhood—
"Ships sail above, underneath walk men
What more surprising there can be then?"

Now I can really see that surprising thing for myself. Trains move under the river while various types of boats and ships sail on it. Many people, carriages, trains etc travel on the bridge built over the river. This, in true sense, appears marvellous to us. Is there anything that these Europeans have not accomplished by the virtue of their Science, skills and hard work? Sir Isenberg Brunnel is the architect of this tunnel. Once he saw a small insect drilling in a piece of wood with its sharp head and making way for itself through it. That gave him the idea that even men can dig tunnels underground with the help of big machines. So he took lesson from that small creature and used his knowledge, wisdom and labour to build the Thames Tunnel.

There is a lot of noise, heavy traffic and many shops on the roads of London, but there is not much entertainment. The British are not fond of conversation and that is why while walking on the road they do not chat or joke. They always walk in a hurry as if they have a train to catch. One cannot see celebrations such as the idol immersion procession after the Durga Puja, the chariot festival, wedding processions, etc on the roads here. Only once a year, they take out a procession on the streets of London to celebrate the appointment of the first magistrate of London which is similar to the wedding processions in our country. The magistrate dressed in an extraordinary fashion rides a magnificent carriage and is accompanied by spectacularly dressed people in carriages as well as pedestrians. The entire entourage goes round parts of London. Apart from this, in some of the roads of London, we can see 'Punch and Judy', which is similar to the puppet dance of our country. But it is much inferior to our puppet dances.

Though London is a big city and is still expanding, various means of transport make commuting from one part of it to another quite fast and inexpensive. England has twenty different railways. Among these, the Northern London railways and the underground railways travel only within and around London continuously. Apart from these there are some very important and some smaller stations in London. If one looks at the railway map of London, it looks like a cobweb. Throughout the day, there is a train at every station at the interval of five or ten minutes so that one can quickly reach from one place to another if one so wishes. In this city, one can move by tram in all the directions. The trams here look like a train. There are cushioned benches inside, on both sides there are glass walls and two doors; there are stairs leading to the roof-top where there are seating arrangements. Twenty-four people can sit in a tram-car.

For the commoners there is another kind of vehicle similar to the tram. It is called an 'omnibus'. People usually call it a 'bus'. They resemble a tram but are smaller in size. They do not move on tracks. It is easier to move around in a bus. These buses are seen plying within and around London. They cover all the important and major roads. In London, about a thousand trams and buses ply every day. Just as there are trams, busses and trains as land transport, there are motor boats to travel through water. Many people go from one part of London to another in these by crossing the Thames without much expense.

Apart from all these means of public transport, there are about five thousand four-wheeled coaches and six thousand five hundred two-wheeled coaches which are for hire. Both these kinds are drawn by a single horse. The four-wheeled coaches resemble the palanquins of our country. Two-wheeled coaches are not found in Bengal but I have seen such in Bombay. It does not accommodate more than two people and opens in the front. When it rains, the glass pane of the window is pulled down and the coach man sits at the back of the carriage instead of the front. There are still many other types of carriages—privately owned ones, shopkeeper's carts, carriages owned by the railway companies, those belonging to the liquor shop owners, and also hand pulled carts. So many of these vehicles ply on London roads that it becomes impossible to keep a count of them.

Here they generally use gas light in all the major public places like roads, shops, theatres etc, and in most of the houses. Nowadays in some places like a few renowned shops, theatres and museums, electric lights can be seen. These are brighter and safer than the gaslights but more expensive too so they cannot be used everywhere. They constantly fluctuate and are not good for the eyes as well. Every evening the main streets of London are illuminated as brightly as the temples of our country. There are lights both inside and outside the shops. When these lights fall on the glass walls and on the shining objects inside the shops their brightness doubles. Thus in winter it is more pleasurable to move about the city in evening than during day time.

BRITISH WOMEN

British women are not all perfect but they have many good qualities. They are very efficient, intelligent and a number of them are educated. Like the men of this country, the women too never neglect their duties. They do not laze away if there is work on hand. When there are no household chores, most of them engage themselves in some useful crafts. Here the men are just bread earners; the responsibility of the household is entirely on the women. Man might be the master of the house, but it is the woman who is truly the queen of the household. They do not have separate 'outer' and 'inner' sections of house as we have in our country. So the women take care of the whole of the house and also have to look after the friends or other guests visiting them. The British women are efficient in running their houses; they watch over all their maids and servants, keep account of household expenses and do whatever is necessary for the proper running of a house. Here mostly the housewives perform all the domestic chores from washing clothes to looking after their children since a maid is neither easily available nor affordable.

Among the affluent there are many women who are completely given to luxury. They leave their home and children to their servants' care and spend their time indulging in music, fashion or reading novels[xxvii]. But how can I blame them for this? In almost every country it is seen that the rich women are lazy. Everywhere, surfeit of wealth is the root cause of a luxurious living. Women build the foundation of a family. So if the women in general had been lazy here, then British household could not have run efficiently and England too would not have developed so much. I feel that they are the true counterparts of their men. The way these women help their men and at times even do men's work are things that we almost never see in our country. Apart from their own work, these women can also execute men's jobs efficiently. They often run shops, work as clerks, teachers, write books and contribute in newspapers, arrange meetings and accomplish much more. Women constitute half of a country's population: their aversion to work and inclination towards laziness harm the whole nation. British women have not restricted themselves to just household chores. They cooperate with men in many other works; great tasks are being accomplished here and there is so much of progress.

British women who live in India are extremely lazy because everything they need, including servants, come quite cheap in this country. Also, they do not care much about money as their husbands earn a high salary. Food, fashion, gossiping, music and strolling in the open air are their chief preoccupations. Taking these women as models, the Indians consider all British women to be babu[xxviii]. There was a time when I too believed that all British women were lazy, but after seeing everything here that impression has changed. I have been greatly surprised to see them capable of as much hard work, tolerance and diligence as men. Instead of just aping the manners of these women if we can imbibe their virtues, then perhaps we shall be truly benefitted.

England provides a lot of opportunity for women's education. There is no dearth of good schools or colleges for girls in cities here. In almost every neighbourhood in London there are two to three girls' schools. Nowadays in the universities of London, Oxford and Cambridge, women can get the same education as men. In the University of London[xxix], women receive education together with men, attending the same classes and under the same professors. They pass the same examinations and receive the same degrees. Though the examinations here are tougher than the B.A and M.A examinations of our country, many women competing with men pass these and often score much higher marks. In London there is no dearth of women who hold university degrees like men. One can often hear names such as Miss Smith, B.A, Misses Jones, M.A, etc. Now women do not hesitate to participate even in those tough examinations which few men take up. This proves that women are not inferior to men in terms of intelligence; the fact that they have achieved as much as men in spite of all the hurdles they face actually prove their superiority. I have heard that in North America, women can attain the high posts of judge, barrister etc, and preside over legal cases as men do. All the upper class women are quite well-educated! The British women yet do not take part in professions that might require higher degrees of efficiency than teaching or practicing medicine. But here too, there is such a progress in the field of education that it seems quite soon the British women will surpass the American ones in this regard.

I cannot express extent of happiness that I feel when I see girls and young women going to schools and colleges in groups like the boys and young men. Here the girls too go to school from the age of six or seven till they are twenty to twenty-five. Many women are not satisfied even with this. Like the educated British men, they continue their pursuit of education till the end of their life. Here there are many women who are authors, scholars and scientists. In certain aspects the women dominate men. Best of the novels of recent times have come from women authors[xxx].

In the provinces girls not only study but also learn stitching, knitting, music, physical exercises and at times even cooking. British parents take good care so that their daughters can learn all these skills. They take equal care to impart education to both their sons and daughters. There is no lack of female teachers here and that is why while appointing teachers for their sons they do the same for their daughters as well, spending almost an equal amount of money for both. Not just in the rich households, but even the daughters of middle class houses pursue education and learn music and other necessary art forms till they are eighteen or nineteen. Parents spend liberally till their daughters become skilled enough in all these subjects. They feel happy to have done their duties towards their daughters. Here the girls belonging to lower classes are much better educated and more intelligent than their counterparts in India. In this country, barring the lowest strata of society, almost everybody's daughters and wives can read, write and play on the piano. Almost everyone is skilled in household chores and dress making etc.

Along with their intellect British women take adequate care of their health. In almost every girls' school there are facilities for physical exercises and games. In many cases, women are as expert as men in games like gymnastics which require physical stamina. They are also at par with men in walking, horse riding, running, and lawn tennis. I have often seen many such women who are stronger than many Bengali men in terms of both physical and mental strength. I doubt whether an Indian man would be able to walk as much as an upper class British woman does. Also, the women here are stronger and more industrious than the women of other European races. It is said that an Italian lady does not walk as much in a year as a British lady walks in a day. So it is not surprising that such strong and industrious mothers will bear healthy and strong children who, will later grow up to be brave, spirited and hard-working British men.

British women on an average are not bad to look at. They have longish but well-shaped face. I have seen many very beautiful women here. Their faces seemed to be carved to perfection. The upper class women have a fair, pinkish and shining complexion which makes them appear so attractive. It is due to their complexion that we often mistake them to be *apsaras*, the court dancers of Indra. But a closer look reveals that though most of them have a beautiful face and a fair complexion, their figure is not attractive and they lack in feminine grace. Most of the women are slim and since they have to work like men and with men that like men they too start lacking in grace. Often their attraction is due to their attire and make-up. Apart from England I haven't seen so much of artificial beauty among women of any other country. Had the Indian women been fair and better attired, they would have been more charming. Another thing that I have noticed is that there are many young women in this country. Either due to cold or due to humidity, English women do not age easily. Often, quite elderly women dress up like the young ones to appear as young as possible.

On reaching England, one is at first quite amazed to see the attire of British women. They love to be extravagant in dressing. Both the rich and the poor are crazy about their clothes. Their craze for dresses is much more than the Indian women's craze for ornaments. Since, it is quite cold here and sunshine is rare, women generally wear black dresses. But even these are of various types and designs. While going out, they almost always wear expensive clothes of the best quality. In summer, their dresses are more fashionable. Nowhere else can anyone come across garments of such different styles and colours. No two women dress alike. But I cannot praise the sartorial preferences of the British women. There are very few whose dresses reflect good taste. Most of the women have no idea of the kind of dresses that look good on them. They use so much of fabric and such countless small accessories to dress themselves while going out that it would seem they have suddenly hit a pot of gold and are now showing off by flaunting these expensive items upon their body. On Sundays, people dress in their best outfit and it becomes difficult to find out their respective social positions by their attire. A few trips to Hyde Park and other similar places frequented by affluent Londoners is enough to show the extent to which these women go to dress themselves up: in their beautifully embroidered velvet hats, costly gowns made of taffeta or silk, different types of British shawls, gloves, gold chain, gold bangles and iron-circlet, they seem to step right out of a picture or a wardrobe to show themselves off. Some of the wealthy wives wear clothes worth not less than two to three hundred rupees.

It is amazing to note the number of artificial accessories these women use to make themselves appear prettier. One shall be amazed to know about the numerous artificial implements the English women use to enhance their beauty. By using corset, crinoline, and other similar items, they alter their figures in such a way that it becomes difficult to make out who is naturally beautiful and who has artificially made herself so. I have heard that they undertake a lot of pain to change their original figure in order to look beautiful. Previously, they used to wear their belts so tight as to look slimmer that they would often fall unconscious while walking on the roads. Nowadays they do not go to that extent. Yet looking at the young women here it seems that they prefer being praised for their good looks to their physical comfort.

There is such an obsession for dressing up here that many women would find no time for eating or for any other chores. Attires determine a person's class here. If any lady comes out in ordinary attire, people look down upon her. On the other hand, if a lower class woman moves around nicely dressed, people mistake her to be a gentlewoman and treat her accordingly. Actually for the British it is not culture but money which is important. An expensively attired woman, irrespective of her class, draws respect from all quarters here. Therefore everyone tries to dress up as elegantly as possible. Husbands and fathers get fed up with their wives' and daughters' demands for more dresses. The pomp and show of dresses here is much more than that of the ornaments in our country. Our men can still get some respite once a piece of jewellery is procured but English men are constantly pestered with demand for clothes. Here at times, I have come across a carpenter's wife so elegantly attired that she can easily be mistaken for a rich man's wife. You might feel sad to see a man in tattered clothes but you will be equally surprised to see his wife in a beautiful dress. What more can be said regarding this; looking around I am convinced that the British women's pathological fascination for clothes has become a terrible vice. It has gone beyond their control.

British women are quite restless by nature and learn to be smart from their childhood. They are not married off at the age of ten as happens in our country. So they do not have to shoulder family responsibilities at that tender age; nor do they become the mistress of the house by the time they are twelve or thirteen. But by interacting with various kinds of people from their childhood, they become clever in a number of ways. Women of no other European country are as sharp and loquacious as them. If you talk to a thirteen or fourteen year old girl of France, Germany or Italy, etc, she will answer you softly and in simple words. But a British girl of the same age will be more skilled in conversation and can surpass anyone at it. Again, if you visit any public place, you will hear more of women's voices than of men. I have not seen any

British girl sitting quietly. They keep on constantly moving their hands, legs or head without any apparent reason. Often, even young ladies behave improperly in public. British women do not know true modesty. Apparels do not determine modesty of a person. Modesty is actually the humility within oneself. A modest woman is one whose personality reflects a humble heart. But I have rarely come across any British woman whose face reflects such comeliness and modesty. At times they behave in such a shameless manner and show such lack of this feminine attribute that all their other positive qualities seem useless.

British women are neither humble nor welcoming by nature. They do not know the conversational etiquettes. Unlike Indian women they will not sacrifice their meals for any unexpected guest. I have heard that in certain houses, if guests arrive, women keep the delicacies aside first for themselves and then serve the rest to the guests. This might be an exaggeration but you will surely never see or even hear of any such thing in our country. Indian women might lack in strength but they are adorned with tender feminine virtues like demureness, modesty, kindness, love, affection, etc.

We do not lag behind other races in terms of all these virtues. Hindu women once possessed spirit and courage and they still do but lack of freedom and education has turned these virtues ineffective. Apathy from men and superstitions within the society are responsible for Hindu women's degradation and misfortune. It is wrong to think that if a woman has strong qualities like courage and spirit, she will lose the tender virtues. Such happens only among the British women.

Since the British women lack modesty or other such qualities they misuse their freedom at times. Many of you will be surprised to know of their husband hunting endeavours. When the girls here reach marriageable age, they go crazy in their search for a husband. You cannot blame them for it. In England, women are greater in number than men and there is no dearth of educated and good-looking women either. Therefore, as in all other aspects, here too there is a tough competition among the young women. On reaching marriageable age every British woman goes crazy over finding the ways to attract men and ascertain that she is preferred over the rest of the women. They frequently visit public places such as roads, gardens, theatres etc which are also frequented by men, and try their best to show off their beauty and other qualities. At this point of life they become more restless and more adept in conversation. They refuse to stay at home and do not care about their parents' wishes. They go everywhere on their own, unaccompanied by any elderly person. I do not think they have any ill intention behind such behaviour but only a desire to get a husband as desired. Like fishermen, the women here spread their nets in the larger areas; if men, like fish, once get caught within these nets, then they will not find any way out of them. Their happiness knows no bound if they can catch a husband before their youth or beauty fades. Those who are ugly have to suffer a lot here. In spite of all their efforts they cannot procure a husband for themselves and have to remain spinster throughout their lives.

Many Indians consider most of the British women to be of dubious moral character, the reason being their free movement in public places such as roads, fields or gardens, and in the presence of men they do not hide their faces behind veils or keep their eyes downcast. For once, if they set aside their prejudices and visit England, they will be rid of their above mentioned misconception. Had the British women not been god-fearing, England could not have progressed so much, nor could have earned so much of love and respect from other civilized races either. Not only the barbaric and wild races but even the civilized and developed ones value *satitva* and consider it to be the chief dharma of any woman. It is not that in England we do not come across any woman who has gone astray but they are outnumbered by the good ones. According to me the *satis* in this country are the real ones because it is easier to boast about *satitva* in a domain that excludes men but those who interact with men treating them as equals, hold conversation and go around with them, yet do not compromise their precious dharma, they are the ones who deserve proper praise and they are the ones who possess a greater strength of mind and dharma.

British women learn self-control from their childhood by going out alone in the world. They learn to maintain their dignity from the examples set by their parents. There is so much of interaction between men and women here that people do not think it wrong to meet or interact with a stranger. In this country, gentlemen and ladies relate to each other as brothers and sisters. Men do not look down upon women but respect them. If anyone misbehaves with women, men come to their aid and punish the offender. Men are physically stronger than women so unless they know how to uphold the dignity of women, women's liberation cannot exist. In this country there are many strict laws against men torturing women. If any man assaults a woman physically or verbally, then he can get harsh punishments.

Indian men are afraid to give freedom to women. They fear that after staying subjugated for such a long time, women have become mentally so weak that they will not be able to conduct themselves properly even if free. Well, this is largely true. If a person is suddenly given freedom after remaining under subjugation for a long time, he will not be able to use or retain it properly. But everyone has to learn at some point of time; a baby does not learn to walk at once. It has to be taught and supported again and again, yet it often falls down. The present condition of women in our country is similar to this situation. They are so weak and have reached such a degraded state that if men do not help them compassionately to stand on their own, their situation will never improve. And if they are not gradually initiated along the road to freedom, they will never learn self-control or become independent. A few women, with their little knowledge and freedom had gone astray: that made our countrymen apprehensive. But does it befit the wise men to judge the entire race of women by a few such examples! No one can gain complete success in any new enterprise; there is bound to be some failure. Instead of being apprehensive if they properly educate women prior to giving them freedom, then we shall realise that Indian women are in no way inferior to the British ones.

British women have always known how to preserve their self-respect and independence. They openly interact with men in public places, play and talk with them and gain various kinds of experiences from their childhood. That is why they do not deify them irrationally or constantly dream of love and happiness as well. They get educated, visit various countries, and listen to the discussions that their fathers and brothers have with their friends on various subjects like politics, administration and other serious issues. Thereby they develop a capacity for serious thinking and learn to discern between the good and the evil. They spend most of their time in domestic chores and reading; so idleness cannot spoil their nature and ruin them. Clearly, it is for these reasons that British women are not easily tempted to go astray. Indian women are famous throughout the world for their *satitva*. We never hesitate a bit to sacrifice our lives for the sake of our *satitva* or to leave this familiar world as a mark of devotion towards our husbands. It is true that one does not get to hear such things in this country but the British women too try their best to retain their *satitva*, the chief dharma of any woman.

There are many eminent women here. You must have heard of the names of the highly educated English women such as Miss Mary Carpenter, Miss Florence Nightingale, Lady Baker, and others. In spite of being single, Miss Mary Carpenter used her intellect and education for the progress of her country. She helped to improve the condition of the prisons and other established institutions. She also helped in establishing many women's organisations. She had founded an organisation for the benefit of those young men arriving in England. It is still functioning and has been very useful. Everyone is aware of her efforts towards women's education in India. There is no such person who is not amazed at the courage and other feminine virtues of Miss Florence Nightingale who stayed at the military barracks during the Crimean wars and nursed the wounded soldiers.

It makes me happy to think of these women who did not get married to be led by others and served this world with their own strength. But in India, let alone spinsters, even the married women do not come forward to serve the country. British women, even if they remain single or become widows, do not consider their lives to be futile. Rather, they try their best to do their duties as human beings. One can achieve a lot with the help of other people, but those women, who singlehandedly and conscientiously work towards the betterment of this world, are rare: we cannot even imagine how precious their lives are.

Among the married British women too there are many who are truly devoted to their husbands and are always by their side. Though there is women's liberation here, there is no lack of faithful women who follow their husbands. Lady Baker is the chief among such devoted wives. She, in spite of being a woman, was courageous enough to accompany her husband and stayed with him in those deserts where even men are scared to go. She too, along with her husband, traversed the dangerous and unexplored deserts of Africa to discover new lakes and rivers: she was her husband's sole companion in that place devoid of any friends and relations. She was endowed with manly qualities like courage and all the virtues associated with a woman. Lady Bracey is another such virtuous woman. She had to face a lot of hardships while sailing with her husband across various oceans for about one and a half years but she did not hesitate. This great woman has immortalised her achievements by writing a number of books on her voyages and other matters. It is entertaining, encouraging and at the same time broadens one's mind.

1

Come sisters! Let's break out of prisons
or counsel our dear brothers
to untie the fetters that bind
the Bengali women's feet

2

Come and see the freedom enjoyed
by British, French and German women
spirited and cheerful in their hearts
they have no reason for humiliating tears.

3

See here, the men do not

neglect women as insignificant
nor like beasts imprison them
confining them to inner quarters.

4

In Europe, wherever I go
I find women equal to men
Contrarily in unfortunate India
her place lies at the feet of men.

5

For how long shall we remain
prisoners in our own abode
ignorant of all that goes on
within India or in the world?

6

Stay happily confined
to a few rooms, your 'andarmahal',
and know nothing beyond household chores
not even who visits the *sadar*[xxxi].

7

Look at the women here
doing domestic chores with care

yet at their leisure and as they wish
they visit a garden or attend meets

8

They are not happy
confined to home; how to be so—
without freedom a life higher
like humans, cannot carry on.

9

We lack that strength of progress,
tied that we are in subjugating chains.
Indifferent, we see not out pains,
and lead on a pleasurable life.

10

Sisters! You possess fine hearts
adorned with *satitva*, humility and respect.
But all these are not enough
quick, assemble your courage.

11

Sisters! Everyone says,
for the weakness of Bengali women
their brothers are hesitant

to allow them independence.

12

So I say, arise and proceed
to chase their misconception away.
Brace yourself up in daring
and dazzle as brilliant as lightning.

13

Sisters! I have cut through bondage
yet find no happiness without you.
Your pale faces and tearful eyes
stays with me, day and night.

14

If you can taste this freedom,
once in your bonded life
you wouldn't wish to remain imprisoned
or keep your faces hidden in veils.

15

There is no shame in uncovered faces.
as we think in our deluded minds.
So I repeat! Wake up you all
in false fears don't waste your lives.

ROYAL PALACE — CLUB — MUSEUM — THEATRE — DRINKING HOUSES

A look at the Royal palaces, great buildings and public places is enough to make one take in the greatness and wealth of London. Here there are a total of eight to nine palaces. Among these, the one in which Queen Victoria resides during her London visit is known as the 'Buckingham Palace'. This palace had been built sixty years back and about a crore and twenty lakh rupees had been spent in building it. Buckingham Palace is situated in the south western part of London. There is vast expanse of garden around it and from a distance it looks like a very high and huge house. But its exterior is not very ornate. Moreover, smoke and dust in London does not let any building retain its whiteness. I do not need to mention in this book the amount of expensive and exquisite items that are there within. Everyone knows that the kings and queens live extravagantly, yet it seems that this palace does not have the splendour suitable for the empress of England.

Among the great edifices of this place, Parliament House is one of the best. It is situated on the bank of the Thames, at a short distance from the Queen's palace. Parliament House is huge and occupies about eight acres of land. It is built of stone and three and a half crore rupees were spent in its construction. Its architecture speaks of skill and expertise. It looks all the more beautiful because it is situated on the river bank. Apart from the House of Lords and the

House of Commons, it also comprises of a library, conference halls for ministers and many other big chambers. There is an ornate throne in the House of Lords, for the Queen at times presides over its proceedings. The parliament remains in session for seven months in a year. To visit the House during that period, we have to seek permission from one of its members. But since there is not much space in the area where common people can sit, very few people get a chance to visit the parliament during that period. When the Parliament is not in session, one can easily enter the House and take a proper look around. Above the parliament roof there are a number of towers and the highest one has a large clock. This clock has four faces on four sides but is controlled by a single machine. As soon as it gets dark, the clock is illuminated from within, so its hands can be seen from far. Its bell can be heard from a distance of four miles during day and from almost all parts of London during night.

The bank of the Thames near the Parliament House has been beautifully paved with stones. There is a path across the river and there are benches along it. The entire pathway is illuminated with electric lamps at night. It is quite pleasant to walk here in the summer evenings and get a nice view of the Thames flowing through London. Hundreds of boats can be seen floating on the river and steamers ferrying people. There is also a well-constructed bridge over it, used by both pedestrians and vehicles. In Calcutta there is only one bridge over the Ganges whereas throughout London, there are seventeen bridges over Thames, each at a distance of about 300 feet from each other. But motor vehicles can use only a few of them. If you look ahead, on the other side of the river, there are many buildings and factories. If you notice properly you can see busy people moving around, engaged in various activities.

Many of you must have heard about a house made of glass situated near London. This 'crystal palace' or the house of glass is located at a distance of about six miles from London. This had been inaugurated in 1854 for the Great Exhibition and more than one and half crore rupees were spent in building it. There is a beautiful garden surrounding the house, spreading across an area of two acres. There are many artificial fountains and waterfalls in this garden. Flowers, creepers and plants of various kinds add to its beauty during summer. It is said that there is no garden bigger and better than this in entire Europe. The building has an ethereal look from a distance. There are glass walls on all sides and glass ceiling which is circular and vaulted with a peak rising from the centre. When the entire palace and the garden are lit up by electric lights, it resembles the palaces described in the *Arabian Nights*, stories which we had read in our childhood. I have heard that nothing apart from glass and iron had been used to construct this structure. Though it is made of glass, it can withstand wind and rain like the buildings made of stone or bricks. Here, there are various kinds of entertainment programmes such as orchestra, short skits and farce, flower shows and animal fairs, every day except Sundays. In summers, beautiful shows of fire crackers are organised in the garden. During summer they also organise wonderful displays of fireworks in the garden. Apart from these, there are fishes in aquarium, toys and various other things worth seeing inside the house.

A number of impressive structures had been constructed under the care of Prince Albert, late husband of the Queen, among which, Albert Hall is quite famous. It is round in shape and so spacious that about eight thousand people can be easily accommodated. It has twenty six doors and at night it is lit up with eight thousand gas lights. Often excellent orchestra performances are organised here. High Court and other important offices in London are much bigger than those in Calcutta but their dull exteriors steal away the elegance. And none of them look better than the beautiful white-washed buildings of our country with their green blinds.

In the western part of London, there are many big buildings, called 'clubs'. These are meeting places for a number of people, but not like the associations that we have in our country. Here there are facilities for reading newspapers and books, eating and even spending a night. There are about fifty clubs in entire London. Among them, the 'Athenaeum Club' is the largest and the most famous. It looks like a palace from outside. There are many beautifully furnished rooms here and attentive, well-mannered servants. This club has all the luxurious amenities found in Europe and all that a gentleman might require. Its library contains around fifty thousand books and a well-constructed, spacious reading-room. Here one can read almost all the newspapers and monthly journals of England and some important newspapers of other countries as well. At night the entire place is brightly illuminated. You can read books or newspapers there whenever you wish to. When hungry, you may eat whatever you feel like; and apart from that, there is space where one can sit and talk with friends, and arrangement for games like billiards, cards, etc. In short, this place has all that one needs for both physical and mental relaxation. These clubs show how fond these British are of their comfort and enjoyment in life. They can readily spend hundreds of rupees for making life comfortable—they cannot lead a life without luxury. To be a member of any of these clubs, one has to pay an annual fee starting from about fifty rupees, going up to three, four or five hundred, depending on the status of that club. Most of these clubs have a large number of members; some of them may have even up to eight hundred or thousand. Not just India, but most of the other countries are yet unaware of this aspect of luxury called clubs. It is quite surprising that in a country like England where people do not like to interact or talk much among themselves one can see so many clubs, societies and 'companies'.

British Museum is one of the prime places to be visited in London. It is situated in the centre of the city. As in the museum of Calcutta, here also there are a number of ancient exhibits. Just near the entrance, on both sides, there are statues of Egyptian, Assyrian and Indian gods and heroes. In front there is a stone carving of Indra and his court at Amravati. Amazing! We neglect these sculptures nowadays, but on a close scrutiny, they reveal a lot about the ancient practice of sculpting, customs, tradition and history. Once all these had been built by the Hindus and preserved by them.

But gradually with the diminishing strength and spirit of the Hindus, they have vanished as well. They have been reassembled here by the industrious British after a lot of hard work.

They have spent a huge amount of money to collect and bring many such ancient and exceptional artefacts from various countries of Asia, Europe, Africa and America. Which Indian will not be curious as well as pleased to know about the kind of armours Hindus wore in the ancient times, the weapons they used in the wars, the kind of clay utensils they used to worship their gods, and the kind of clothes and various other things that they used? Here, apart from the ancient objects, one can also get to see many extraordinary items related to science, art, and literature. Previously, this place also housed bones and skeletons of animals from various countries as well as their models made of burnt straw. But now they have been shifted to another museum.

Apart from all these there is also a very good library and reading room in the British Museum. Previously, people here could only see the collection and appreciate; but now, after the reading room was built in the year 1856, people can also read whatever they wish to, without a fee. The museum has an astonishing collection of books in terms of variety, subjects and languages. Till now they have around two crore books and this number is increasing every year. I have heard that the National Library in Paris, the capital of France, contains more books than the British Museum, but there they do not have such fine reading arrangements or such diversity of collection of books. The reading-room is very spacious. It can accommodate about five hundred people. It is round in shape. The dome-shaped ceiling is made of opaque glass. The counter for issuing and returning books is in the centre of the room where the library staff is also present. The seats for the readers are around that area, so that no seat is far from the centre. There are three tiered shelves along its walls holding numerous books. For every reader there is a chair and a table which is blocked at front so that the reader can read undisturbed. The tables and the leather covered chairs are very clean. On each of the tables there is space for keeping inkpot, ink, blotting paper, brush to wipe pen and a place for keeping hat. Every seat has a number. The reader has to write the name of the book he wants to read, its number according to the book catalogue, the name of its author, his own name and his seat number on a piece of printed paper and give it to the office at the centre of the room. After sometime one of the attendants of the library brings that book to the reader. One person can borrow more than one book in this way. The reader remains responsible for the book he issues till he returns that to the counter and takes back the slip. Some seats are reserved exclusively for women, though they also sit on any of the other seats too. No one below the age of twenty-one is allowed to use this library. Even then only those who come with a reference and belong to the gentry are allowed to read here.

Apart from the British Museum, there are seven or eight other museums in London. Among them, South Kensington Museum is comparatively more famous. Here they have many art and craft objects. Other museums are not as big or famous as these.

In Calcutta, there are only two or three hospitals but London has sixteen big ones. All of them have patients to their maximum capacity and they run on charity. It is not possible to count the number of big or small churches that are there in London. If one starts counting, the number may go up to about five hundred churches in entire London. Two important ones are the Saint Paul's Cathedral and the Westminster Abbey.

Saint Paul's Cathedral has a fine architecture. It took about thirty-five years to be completed and an amount of eighty lakh rupees was approximately spent. It is 510 feet high, 240 feet in breadth and 2100 feet wide. The roof of the church is shaped as a high dome and above it there is a tower, about 375 feet high from the ground. This church can be seen from quite a distance and one can easily view the entire city of London from its top. There is a whispering room within the church where even a barely audible whisper can be clearly heard as it is echoed throughout the room. Westminster Abbey is built differently and its exterior is very beautiful. It is much smaller than the Saint Paul's Cathedral. Inside it, there are tombs and monuments of the important people of England.

There are about thirty theatres in London; they have daily performances, except on Sundays. A few theatres can accommodate even up to four hundred people. Most of the theatres are well built and beautifully decorated. There are so many different types of plays and farcical performances going on in London that one cannot keep a count of it. And most of these theatres are generally crowded. God knows from where so many people visit these! Apart from theatres, there are a number of big music halls which organize orchestras of superior quality. London also has a number of opera houses where mostly singing performances are organized. At times there are some other kinds of musical performances too. But I have heard that in such houses people indulge in drinking and it is frequented by people of all kinds—both good and bad.

Apart from theatres, auditoriums and opera houses, there are many other smaller places of entertainment here. Anyone who has money need not worry about entertainment in London. Whether one is young or old, woman or man—everyone has places to visit for recreation. Among the smaller places of entertainment here, there is one that is quite interesting. It is a room which contains statues of famous people from past and present times. These are made of wax. The figures of the king, queen and other great people are beautifully embellished. They have such beautiful colour and form that in dim light, they appear to be living people. Here there is a room known as the 'Hall of Horrors' which has the figures of all notorious murderers, crooks etc. Among these there is also the statue of Nana Sahib of our country. I do not know whether Nana Sahib actually looked like that or not. But whatever his looks might have been, the British considered him to be a dangerous murderer. That is why his statue has a place here. This place was first opened by a French woman and since then it is running under her name,

'Madame Tussaud'. In the museum there is a fine statue of that lady as well. I think they can maintain these wax statues here because England is a cold country. In our country, all these would have melted.

There is no dearth of hotels in London. People can select them according to their pockets. In some hotels, the expense is three rupees per day, and in some other, it is ten. Some hotels are quite huge—about eight to ten floors high and of similar width. There are five to six hundred rooms inside. Some are even bigger than the queen's palace. Here there are many shops where one can go at anytime of the day and eat anything one wishes to. While on road or if there is some problem at home, a person can go to these places and eat cooked food. Though it is more expensive to eat there, it is easier and more convenient. Such shops are known as 'restaurant'. This is a French word and this facility of eating out has come from France.

In this chapter, I have talked about many big buildings, palaces, etc, and now I shall wind up after telling you about the houses that have been dedicated to *suradevi*[xxxii]. These liquor shops are known as 'public houses'. They also sell 'gin', 'brandy', etc, so people also call them 'gin palace'. In London there are about six thousand licensed liquor shops. Apart from that there are various other places where common people can drink. Here, there are more liquor shops than churches and there is no such locality where a couple of public houses cannot be seen. These shops are quite big and they remain open till late at night as compared to other shops. All other shops are shut by nine or ten pm but these remain open till about midnight. Huge glass windows and the bright gas lights outside these shops dazzle the eyes. These streets are brightly lit and if you glance inside, even the interior looks as bright. Beautiful chandeliers of gas lights hang from the ceiling and various other decorative lights adorn the walls. There is well polished, fashionable furniture and the counter top is made of marble. A few young girls, fair and beautifully dressed, sit behind these counters and sell alcohol in small quantities costing a few pennies; in some places young men or boys are also employed to do this job. In front of the table many poor and ugly men in shabby clothes are found to be standing and drinking. Some spend their entire money in drinking, some hurl abuses under its influence and still others engage in quarrels. Men and women with ugly appearances throw themselves at suradevi's feet. In many liquor shops, people indulge in bitter fights and even commit murders. It is really surprising that the public houses situated in these hideous and extremely poor localities are becoming increasingly glamorous each day.

BRITISH MARRIAGE AND DOMESTICITY

In England, both men and women marry according to their choices and their parents do not create any problem by forcing them to marry someone else. The marriageable age in this country is between twenty to thirty years for women and twenty-five to thirty-five for men. But many of them marry quite late as well. Men do not marry till they have a decent earning. Neither the rich, nor the poor marries till he has saved enough wealth needed to run a family. People in our country have children and even grandchildren by the age these English people get married. Due to early marriage and weather condition in India people look old at quite an early age; but here, that is the age when they step into real youth and get the first experiences of joys and sorrows of a conjugal life.

England does not have the concept of match making or match makers, as we have in our country. Young men and women find their own beloved. This period of choosing one's love is known as 'courtship period'. Young men and women assemble at some public gathering or friends' place; and after a few such meetings they come to know each other. Gradually, some men might develop a liking for some women. This is the first step of British love. It is the man who first speaks of his feelings or writes a letter to the lady he likes. If the lady has similar feelings, she accepts his proposal. After expressing their mutual feelings in this manner, they start seeing each other at public spaces. They meet as often as possible and try to understand each other. They spend at least two to three months in this way. Later, if neither of them has any objection and both like each other; the man proposes marriage to the woman. If the woman accepts that proposal, they decide to get married and do not wait for their parents' approval. In no other European country, does the man or the woman dare to raise the question of marriage without the prior consent of their parents.

When both the British man and woman agree to get married, they inform their parents. Usually parents do not object to their wards' wish and give their consent. The sons and daughters here decide to get married at quite a grown-up stage and after many careful considerations, so why should not the parents agree to their choice? After receiving the consent of their parents, the young man and the woman take the pledge to get married. This is quite similar to our custom of the *patra* or the final marriage contract as agreed upon by both the families. After this pledge, both are legally bound to get married to each other. This pledge is known as 'engagement' and after this engagement, both the man and the woman wear a ring; this is known as the engagement ring. Though people here select their life partners themselves, one can at times hear about breaking off an engagement. If after being engaged, the man refuses to marry the woman, then the woman can complain against him and if she wins the case, the man has to pay a heavy penalty.

After getting engaged, they behave as future man and wife towards each other. Together they go to church, watch plays and visit various other places. This period is called the courtship period and this courtship can extend from about six months to even six years in certain cases. I have already said that the British do not get married until it is convenient for them in all possible ways; that is why, many of them, even after making all the arrangements regarding marriage, have to wait for it due to financial constraints or some other problem. When it becomes opportune from all quarters, only then they decide their wedding day and proceed towards their marital life. The British too respect the sanctity of marriage and consider it to be a sacred bond of human life. They do not support infidelity and even men consider it to be a serious offence.

In every country there are a lot of festivities on the day of wedding. The delight of the family members and specially the young ones knows no bound. Here, the bride and the groom enjoy the most because unlike in India, here, they are not children. Both of them know each other, so they are neither apprehensive nor tensed. In this country, wedding takes place not at the bride's place but at the church, in the morning. On that day the rich people decorate their houses and church with flowers, garlands and bouquets. Flowers are appreciated in every country and since these are natural and pure adornment, all over the world people decorate their houses with flowers during weddings. As in our country, there is no splendour of *barjatri*, the procession with which the groom arrives at the wedding along with his friends and family. Only a few rich ones go to the church in grand cars. Here, instead of *cheli* or the wedding sari, the girl wears a new white dress and the groom wears something nice and new.

Both wear white gloves, have a bouquet in their hands and the girl's face is covered with a white veil. Just as we have *neetkanya* and *neetbor*, a small girl and a boy dressed similar to the bride and the groom; here too, the groom's brother or a close kin dresses as his best man and the bride's sister, sibling or cousin, dresses as the bride's maid. The bridegroom has only one best man but the bride can have up to twelve brides' maids, depending on their affluence. They too dress in new clothes like the bride and the groom, and all the brides' maids cover their faces with a white veil as a sign of good omen, wear white gloves and hold a bouquet.

Everyone gathers at the church and the wedding takes place at the appointed hour. The bride and the groom stand near the altar and exchange marriage vows in the presence of the priest and all their friends and relatives, that they accept each other as husband and wife, that they will not part till their death, etc, etc. Then both of them pray to God and seek His blessings. The priest reads selected portions from the Bible, gives advice to the new couple and prays to the Almighty for their well-being. Parents and other guests also participate in this prayer. As in India, here too, the father, uncle or elder brother gives away the girl to the bridegroom. After the promise and prayer the bride and the groom go to another room along with the priest and elders and sign their names in the registration book. Two more people sign their names there as witnesses. Taking marriage vows at the altar of God gives religious sanction to the wedding; similarly registration makes it legally valid. Once the wedding ceremony is over the husband and wife comes out of the church. According to the custom here, guests sprinkle rice upon the newly wedded couple and hit the bridegroom with shoes. This ritual of beating the bridegroom with shoes is similar to the ritual of boxing his ears in our country. But in Bengal, at times, they box the ears so tightly that the bridegroom, who is just a boy, starts crying. In this country, they hit him with very soft, velvet shoes, which instead of hurting him, gives him pleasure. From the church, everyone goes either to the bridegroom or the bride's father's house and enjoy the wedding feast with their friends and relatives.

Like the iron bangle of our country, a white gold ring is the symbol of wedding here. After the wedding ceremony is over, the bride takes off her engagement ring and wears this wedding ring. The old and superstitious women of this country consider taking the wedding ring off one's hand to be an ill omen. There is also an advantage of wearing this ring— a look at a woman's hand will let one know about her marital status. In this country too, in some of the wedding rituals, one can get glimpses of a few superstitions. Such rituals are observed only by the less educated or uneducated women. Girls' fathers in this country, unlike their French and Indian counterparts, do not have to gift a lot of jewellery, dresses or money to their daughters on the occasion of the wedding. One may gift a large amount of cash or various items if one so wishes, but it is not a compulsion. Parents and friends of the newly-wedded gift them various items, watch, chain, books, clothes, etc. just as we do in our country.

The newly wedded couple goes to some secluded place for a few weeks to enjoy themselves. This period, immediately after marriage, is known as 'honeymoon'. Perhaps, this period of life, just after marriage, is the happiest time of life and that is why it has such a sweet name. This is the stage when the new couple is ignorant of any problem that might come in their conjugal life, such as those pertaining to household, children or the servants and maids, etc. They consider conjugal life to be only blissful. Many couples spend even two to three months in this way, enjoying their love for each other. Worries of a worldly life do not touch them. After that, the couple returns home to start their life together.

In this country, an unmarried woman is addressed as a 'miss' and the married one as 'mistress' or 'misses' in short. Many think that the names of the British women change after marriage, but actually that's not so. Just as we name our babies during the rice-eating ceremony, celebrating the baby's first meal of rice, British do that during baptism. Parents choose the names for their children. That name is called the Christian name and it never changes. After marriage, only the surname, which she got from her father's side, gets changed. Just as in our country if one Kumari Nirmala Dutt is wedded to one Mr. Mitra, her name changes to Srimati Nirmala Mitra; in their country too a Miss Smith whose name is Rose, when wedded to another Mr. Allen becomes Mrs. Rose Allen. Marriage between first cousins from either of their parents' sides is allowed among the British. They have no misgivings regarding such marriages within family. But surprisingly, unlike our country, here a person cannot marry the sister of his deceased wife. Many people have been trying to change this system but have not been successful yet.

After marriage neither men nor women stay in their parents' house. They set up a new household. The conjugal life here is very different from that of our country. Here, except when the husband is at work, the couples stay together. They take their meals together, go out together as well as have discussions on their household, religion and many other things of this world.

Why do people marry? People all over the world, including India would reply in one voice that is it to gain a constant companion in good times and bad, a helpmeet and a partner to share the worries of life. I have no doubt that the women of this country truly fulfill these requirements of their husbands. Men and women share their happiness and sorrows equally, pray together and the wife often helps her husband in various jobs. If the husband becomes incapable of working, many a times, the wife works hard to earn to support her husband and children.

It is true that to us, the British conjugal life appears to be happy and blissful. The couple shares both their happiness and hardships in good times and bad. The husband while going on a pleasure trip or recreation never leaves his wife behind. He is not happy to spend all that he earns only on himself, rather, tries his best to keep his wife happy as well. On every Sunday, men and women go to the church together to pray, read from the Bible, and sing psalms. The husband, though wise himself, seeks his wife's advice in whatever he undertakes. The wife too is quite intelligent. She does not consider her husband to be her lord, but her beloved; and therefore tries to keep him happy by showering all her love on him. The English men do not seek pleasure outside their homes as their wives, who are quite educated, provide them with fit companionship. We can say that the British women are their husbands' right hand. They often provide good advice to their husbands and the husbands are equally happy and eager to accept them.

I feel depressed whenever I think of the challenges in the conjugal lives of the couples in our country. The wife, confined at home, does not know how her husband spends his entire day and the husband too does not know the way his wife spends her time. The mistress is scared of the master of the house. The babus sit in their lavishly decorated drawing-rooms where they smoke hookah, play cards and chat with their friends or they go out for walks. But the women of the house remain enclosed within, occupied with household chores only. The wife loves her husband and tries her best to prepare good food for him and to look after his comfort; but the husband does not treat his wife in a judicious manner. She too does not know how to treat him properly. Very few people in our country understand the actual relationship that should exist between a man and his wife. And one cannot put much blame on the men and women either; the root cause behind these are the superstitions, the evil practices of our society, child marriage and the improper conduct of the parents towards their children. Though Indian women are extremely chaste, all these factors come in the way of their mutual happiness.

Though there is proper love and affection between majority of married couples in England, or a long courtship period before marriage, the number of cases of separation filed by the husband or wife is also more here than in any other country. If the husband tortures his wife or commits adultery, she can easily take him to court and seek separation. Similarly, the husband too can leave his wife if she violates her chastity. And after being separated in this manner, they can once again marry according to their wishes. In our country, there is provision for leaving one's wife but one does not get to hear of any wife leaving her husband. Even if the husband has hundreds of faults or is adulterous, the Hindu wife, devoted to him, will bear everything in silence. She will be ashamed to file a suit against her husband and consider it a despicable task. In this country, both the men and women consider it a serious offence and also a sin to break one's trust after marriage. Here the husband cannot always act according to his wishes only. I had a notion that the British people are not very caring or affectionate towards their children. It is true that they do not live in joint families and their love for the foreigners is a fake one. But I do not any longer believe that there is no affection between parents and their children. British parents take proper care of their children till the latter learn to look after themselves or set up a family of their own. The parents put in their best efforts to teach their children to live independently when they grow up. In this aspect I think, the parents in this country are more considerate than those of our country. When the children grow up, they do not become a burden to their parents. Instead, they live in separate houses. Hence, there is not too much of intimacy between them. But that does not mean that all love and affection among them is completely lost. Whenever they wish to, they meet and enjoy a meal together. Unlike in our country, here the domestic quarrels are quite infrequent, so people have a congenial relationship with parents, children or siblings throughout their lives. Hindus have too much of parental affection and at times it seems superfluous but often the parents there are not appropriately dutiful towards their wards. Also, the horrible incidents of family dissensions that are heard at times have no parallel in this country.

When the British children come of age, parents treat them as friends. When the children do something according to their own choice, unlike the Indian parents, the parents here do not brand them as 'disobedient' and thereby make their as well as their children's life miserable. Parents understand that once their children reach their youth, they develop an ability to distinguish between the right and the wrong. That is when they do not want to follow their parents' wishes in everything they do, as they did in their childhood. So the parents advise their grown-up sons and daughters to act with self-discretion. They do not consider it beneath their dignity to take advice from their children; on the contrary, they often consult them regarding various matters. Children too are not afraid of their parents or do not hate them as insensitive or uneducated. They always maintain a respectful and proper attitude towards their parents. If the parents are in the wrong and their children try to correct them, the parents do not get into a fit of blind rage; rather, they try to analyse if such suggestion is rational and act accordingly. Considering such a relationship between parents and their wards, who will not consider the domestic life among the British to be a happy one?

Here, the way siblings behave towards each other is very different from that in our country. From early childhood, brothers and sisters grow up together in a similar way. Brothers do not hate their sisters just because they are girls, nor do they look down upon them. On growing up, they come even closer. Parents are equally attentive towards their sons' and daughters' education and treat them at par. Both the son and the daughter, one being the heir to the family and a bread earner and the other about to be sent to another family are not differentiated by the parents. Therefore, brothers and sisters grow up both wishing well for the other. And irrespective of their ages, they talk to each other, read books, go out or play together. In this country, quarrel or difference of opinion among brothers and sisters is almost absent. There is a loving relationship not just among the unmarried siblings; it continues even after they are married. The brother and sister get busy with their respective families, yet whenever they can manage, they meet each other with all warmth and affection.

In England, only the eldest son can inherit paternal property. The father, during his lifetime, can bestow his other children with some money or property but after his death, no one apart from the eldest son can have any right to his property. This system has both its positive and negative aspects. It seems to be a matter of grave injustice that only the eldest son will be the heir to the entire property and no one will get anything else. The fact that the eldest son inherits everything simply because he is lucky to be a first born in spite of being lazy and uneducated must hurt the other siblings. If the father meets with sudden death, his other children become very poor and helpless. It is often seen that the eldest son, having inherited his father's property leads a lavish life while the younger ones lead a life of poverty and hunger. One positive aspect of this system is that, since only the eldest son is entitled to property, younger ones do not file any case to inherit maximum amount of it, neither do they have any intention to do so.

So relationship between brothers is not marred with quarrels, debates or envy. All the other sons, leaving the eldest one, engage in pursuit of livelihood from an early age. They know that in spite of being sons of a rich father, they will need to earn for their own families. So they learn to become self-dependent and carve out their own path in life. Existence of such a system ensures that property is not wasted and only one of the sons might grow up to be lazy while the rest work hard to earn their living. But in our country almost all the sons of a rich man grow up to be idle and they waste their assets by filing court cases against each other.

But again, it is this very system that makes the people selfish. Everyone wants to live independently. Each grownup son wants to live on his own, in a separate house. Instead of living in a joint family with a number of people, each wants to live only with his wife, children and servants. Often, they are concerned just with themselves and what belong exclusively to them and do not wish to maintain any contact with their other relations. This is very much prevalent among the common people. The father is least perturbed by the problems that his son might be facing. Since they are not bothered by the hardships of their close relatives there is no question of their feeling anything for people not related to them.

Well, the cultured people of England have a wonderful lifestyle. All the members of the family take their meals together. From the youngest son of the family to the father, all sit around the same table. Before eating, the head of the family stands near the table and says a prayer while the rest listens to him quietly. This prayer is known as 'grace'. This is done to thank the Lord for the food they eat and to seek his blessings. Together the family members entertain themselves and chat with each other. Men and women of the family take their food and spend time together, the young ones learn courtesy and good conduct from their childhood. They treat even the servants of the house as their children and take care of their physical as well as mental growth. The servants too respect their masters and are devoted to them.

The rich people in this country maintain seven to eight servants—a cook, a kitchen maid, two to three maids for household chores, a maid for the lady of the house, a coachman and a butler. In some houses there are even fifteen to eighteen servants. The chief among them is called 'butler'. He is in charge of the overall supervision of the house, the keys and wine-cellar. He is held responsible if something gets stolen from the household. The lady's maid oversees the work of other servants. She is responsible for the store room and other items. In most of the houses there are only maidservants. Here, only the rich can afford to keep a male help. The salary of a male domestic help is almost thrice that of a maid plus there is a tax for keeping him. In this country, most of the servants are unmarried and young—within age group of twelve to thirty five years. The salary of the maid servants ranges from rupees eight to rupees twenty or twenty-five a month. The male servants' salary varies from rupees twenty-five to rupees fifty or sixty per month.

Those people who can maintain about eight maidservants in our country cannot keep more than two or three here. Here the maids have to work quite hard and they do all sorts of jobs. They keep the entire household clean, do the dusting, make the beds, water the plants, polish the shoes, go to the market, act as doorkeeper, etc. Work of one maidservant here is equivalent to that of three in our country. They do not get any rest from seven o'clock in the morning till ten or eleven at night. In this country, the servants are also as sincere towards their duty as everyone else. Nobody has to rebuke them constantly to make them work. The mistress of the house has to only assign them their respective tasks. The servants consider such admonitions quite disgraceful; therefore they complete their task in time without any supervision. Well there might be a few among them who are not as good but majority of the British servants are very efficient, hard working, intelligent and trust worthy. Their only fault is that they love to be independent; unlike the servants in other countries, they do not like to be controlled at all times. And once their work is over, like their employers, they too like to dress up and go out.

In many respectable households, servants are included as a part of the family during religious services. The master of the family attends the Sunday prayers with his wife, children, friends and servants. The entire family along with their guests gathers to read aloud from their holy books and pray to the Almighty. Generally, the master of the house plays the part of the priest. The pious atmosphere that prevails within the family during such times is wonderful. All the members either kneel down or sit with bowed head, facing the wall. Finally, the master reads out the precepts one after another and the rest of the family discusses those. At the end of the prayer, the servants one by one leave the hall solemnly, and the family spends time as they wish to.

Upon observing all these things it seems to me that though British are quite selfish, their domestic life is much better and happier than that of many other races. Though they are not very social, they enjoy domestic bliss. They do not care much for the mindless foppery. The only thing they understand is their own comfort and that is their chief goal. They lead a lavish life-style if they own a house and possess a lot of money. A British, who spends most of his lifetime in a cold and desolate climate, considers a few things to be of great comfort. He loves to sit near the glowing fireplace in a clean and fine house of his choice, with all the doors and windows closed and indulge in sweet chitchats with his devoted, pleasing and well decked up wife. He likes to see the smiles on the rosy faces of his well brought-up, neat and clean children. He also cherishes a neatly decorated and well furnished house which will have both necessary and luxurious items. The British, howsoever rich they might be, do not cause disgrace in the family by indulging in licentiousness or other evils. Every British gentleman firmly believes in the sanctity of home. His domestic life is so pleasant and rewarding because he keeps his home happy and honourable.

WINE OR POISON

Every Indian knows about the British love for alcohol[xxxiii]. No other race can consume as much alcohol as the English or behave in such a beastly manner after getting drunk. Here, even the person who earns fifty paisa a day goes to the liquor shop once or twice a day. As soon as you step out of the house you will get to see how much alcohol they can consume. There are public houses all along the roads. I have already described these liquor shops, now I shall talk about the effects of alcoholism.

There are many educated people in England and nowadays the British are also earning a lot by exploiting other nations. Then why does England have so many poor people? And why are the poor so miserable here? It is not possible to provide an immediate answer to these questions. But gradually one can see, hear and understand that this unavoidable poverty is the result of consuming alcohol and it is under its effect that the poor people of this country behave in such a beastly manner. Previously, this habit was so rampant here that one would often come across rich people or members of the royal family rolling on the roads after getting heavily drunk. Fortunately, now this vice is much less prevalent among the gentry and we hardly come across them behaving in such a horrible manner. But among the poor it is same as ever. It is said that after getting drunk, the French talk a lot, the Germans sleep and the English fight. And truly, once drunk, they lose both their conscience and humanity.

The poor people of England, once drunk, hurl horrible abuses, beat up their wives and children, and even kill them at times.

A few months back the newspapers and magazines of this country were largely engaged in a major campaign regarding the wretched condition of the poor and the reason behind it. During that period, there were such horrifying reports on ill effects of drinking habit that it sent shudders down the spine. I do not want to exaggerate anything in this book; rather I shall describe this abhorrent matter in as little words as possible. And in order to let you know what the British themselves think regarding this evil, I am presenting an excerpt of a true incident as recorded in the popular newspaper, 'Daily News'.

The lower class British people earn enough; yet they lead a very miserable and abominable life. The two main reasons behind it are their habit of excessive drinking and extravagance. Such an enormous number of people drain out their money on alcohol that it seems that none will ever be able to save them from their miserable predicament. Moreover in London and other cities there is so much of temptation that it is not surprising that the feeble-minded poor would give in to the addiction of alcohol. Even those who do not have money for food or clothes, pawn whatever little they possess to buy drinks. Living the way they do, an entire family squeezed in a single room in East London and other areas, it is not at all surprising that they would be enticed by the resplendent alcohol shops. Brandy, gin, beer come at a much cheaper price than other luxury goods. So the poor can procure this false enjoyment at a cheap price and gradually get completely addicted. Often, they rush to these attractive shops displaying rows of liquor bottles and consume this poisonous nectar to forget the sorrows and hardships of their wretched lives. Among the middle class too there are many who initially visit these shops once in a while but then they get so addicted that they have no other option apart from succumbing to the temptation of these 'public houses'.

The poor of this country waste one-fourth of their income just on alcohol. Saturdays are particularly horrible here. The poor people get their wages on this day and visit the public houses. As long as they have money to spare they linger here. A public house on a Saturday earns more than the collective earning of all other shops along the same road. If you take a look inside, you will see a frightening crowd of masons, labourers, porters, sweepers and all other low class people shouting and drinking. Alas! Their life would not be so hard if they spend their money to procure food and clothes for their hungry and shabbily dressed wife and children instead of wasting them on alcohol. Not just men, but even women can be found drinking. Grandmother, mother and daughter with a baby in her lap can be found drinking together in a public house. The octogenarian grandmother behaves like a young girl and the infant is just two months old. All of them, except the baby are so heavily drunk that calling them dipsomaniac would not be an exception. Here, you see four generations at a queue in a liquor shop and each of them looking awful and dirty. At times the mother pours some gin down the throat of her baby and says; 'let my baby too get a taste of this.' At this, the already inebriated father laughs hideously and appreciates his wife, saying, 'well, well'. Such horrible and frightening scenes are not to be seen anywhere apart from England.

At midnight, on a Saturday if you visit a public house in a poor neighbourhood, you will find the shopkeeper trying to forcefully evict the inebriated ones out of his shop at the closing time. Drunken men roll on the floor here and there— either unable to get up or not wishing to. Gradually, after being shoved out of the shops, these wretched ones walk down the road in faltering steps. Some fall down on their way and hurt their faces and heads. And once they reach home after many attempts, they instantly pick up a fight with their equally intoxicated wives. Some spend nights on streets; and if any of their kin or the poor wife does not take them home, they often die due to cold.

The saddest part here is that the poorest ones are the worst addicts. It is not possible to pen down the detestable and horrifying incidents that constantly occur here as a result of their alcoholism. If you enter the by-lanes of East London after the shops are closed, you will come across such horrible scenes which are impossible to even bear sights of. One can see women lying about and rolling here and there, their features almost distorted, all either shouting in a filthy language or singing; and drunken men embracing each other in a ghoulish manner. When a man and woman meet, the situation becomes more appalling. It begins with quarrels and abuses and ends in fights or even murders. In certain places, you can hear terrible screaming from one of the nearby houses. Perhaps the drunken husband, after beating his wife, had pushed her down the stairs or smashed her head with a stick. The half-dead wife groans in pain and the neighbours cry out 'murder'. Their shrieks pierce the silence of the night and aims straight at the heart. Here you can see women in frenzy; some madly running after their drunken husbands. A few women can be found lying in a pool of blood, unable to move by themselves. They scream their hearts out. After watching such scenes it seems that these people are inhuman. But this is not the end, worse things happen here.

Many wealthy men having lost all their money under the influence of alcohol are finally forced to live among the poor. Many educated men such as doctors, clergymen, teachers et al, too fall prey to this evil and become so degraded that they are eventually forced to sell matchboxes worth a penny or two on the roads or go begging to make a living. Blessings of suradevi have ruined many a rich men in such a way that they are now reduced to almost begging on the streets under the guise of selling flowers or singing. In some places, men, women and children of a family are forced to live in a single room which is so filthy that it resembles a kennel or a pen. It is not possible to keep a track of the number of wealthy and middle class people who had been reduced to this wretched and helpless state. Among these alcoholic destitute, there are women who once belonged to rich and noble families.

The news or sight of the poor makes us genuinely sad but the well to do British stays detached from them. They are busy in the pursuit of their selfish interest and pleasures and do not bother to care about the hardships of these unfortunate ones. They do spend a lot of money in various good deeds but they do not help the poor. Often they are ignorant of the latter's problems because all such horrible incidents happen only in the locality of the poor and never in the areas inhabited by the gentlemen. I have also mentioned earlier that the upper class British men detest the poor. Even the middle class does not pay any attention towards them. Such great influence of alcohol is not found in any other country of this world and therefore nowhere is the poor so beastly. Particularly, in no other country women get drunk in such an obnoxious manner. Unfortunately today, alcohol is corrupting even a sacred country like India. Nowadays, the rich men of our country are getting drawn towards alcohol. Even the educated young men do not hesitate to imitate the British habit of drinking. I hope they become conscious after reading this section and take it as a warning.

Many people say that without alcohol it is not possible to remain healthy in England. I completely disagree with it—drinking is just a habit. Nowadays, one can find a number of British men who completely abstain from alcohol. And the rate of drinking has considerably reduced among the rich gentlemen of that country. This has not harmed them in anyway, rather it has helped them. In many houses here, the guest is offered liquor and cigar just as we offer beetle leaf and tobacco in our country. It might offend the host if the guest refuses it. So an Indian has to drink at times even against his wishes. But that does not mean that one has to drink habitually or get drunk after reaching England. The aforesaid custom of welcoming one's guest by offering him a drink has greatly reduced among the educated class of England and the habit of drinking is also decreasing among the people. If, even then the educated young men of our country indulge in this habit, it is a matter of grave sorrow.

INTERIOR REGION OF ENGLAND—FARMERS AND LANDLORDS—WEATHER

Just as the buildings and factories cover the cities of England its villages are beautifully adorned with greenery all around. When you leave the city you will see lush green fields on both sides of the road separated from each other by hedges, its beauty enhanced by an occasional big tree. Consistent monotonous sight vexes human minds. A look at these trees, few and far between makes me think that the Almighty had placed them as such to spare us that monotony. Far off one can see few huts of the farmers. Apart from those, every other visible object is green—the place seems to be covered with various kinds of plants, shrubs and creepers. Look around this place from an elevated area and the entire place will appear the same. As far as you can see you will find only vast expanse of green fields. There are no forests here but some patches which are full of useful plants such as "root", "clover", "hop" etc and small bushes. At times you can also find a narrow yellowish stream flowing through a serpentine course. It makes the adjoining fields extremely fertile and hence there is a dense growth of grass there. Huge cows, sheep and various other cattle graze about, ruminate or simply play around here. In England cattle are so healthy and strong because there is a lot of fodder available for them. Various types of food grains and vegetables, chiefly, barley, wheat, potato, cauliflower etc. occupy the major portion of the cultivated land here.

When we visit these fields, far away from the crowd, we forget the beauty of the British cities and discuss the comely beauty of nature that we see here. Whichever way we look, we can see greenery all around. Such sights are delightful and soothing to our eyes. These green stretches of land covered with plants and climbers are called 'meadows'. Apart from the meadows, one can also see some uncultivated land here. The British call them 'commons'. Men have not yet destroyed the natural beauty of these places by agriculture or constructions. Here the surrounding is quiet and lonely; only one or two horses can be seen grazing at a distance but no other animals. These 'commons' are not similar to the uncultivated forestlands of our own country. There are no wild animals here and while walking through this, one need not be scared of snakes or any other creature. Only grass and some small wild plants grow here and the soil is very hard and uneven. Previously, almost the entire land of England was as tough as these areas. I am thrilled to even think of the amount of patience and hard work that the British must have required to make this land arable: but the forbearance and perseverance of the British have helped them achieve success in this difficult task. In every century they turn hundreds of acres of more inferior forest lands into beautiful fields and eventually cultivate them to yield various kinds of produce.

While strolling through the fields you might face a short spell of rain every couple of hours. But the landscape looks so beautiful after the shower that we are not bothered by that inconvenience. The grass looks fresher and greener. On tiny leaves, there are shining water droplets, just about to trickle down, looking like bright pearl strings. As the sun re-emerges from the clouds, the fields look brighter. Small white and yellow flowers on the grass look more beautiful as they reflect the sun rays. Sometimes you can see breathtaking scenes taking shape in the grey sky overhead. The sky, most of the time remains covered with dull, dark clouds, some moving at a speed and some others still. Gradually, the clouds in motion come and envelop the stationery ones. Almost immediately the latter slide away and appear to rise their hoods in the manner of trampled serpents. In quick succession, another cloud comes to occupy the vacant space. Like this, one after the other, the clouds cover the entire sky in layers similar to stairs. Shortly, another group of clouds resembling a huge grey elephant move swiftly across the sky. The layers of cloud scatter and rush here and there and eventually, this huge cloud bursts into rain, disturbing the beautiful sight.

The huts in rural parts of England look extremely poverty-stricken. From a distance, they remind me of the farmers' shacks of our country. These huts have walls made of mud and wood and a very low thatched roof. The rooms are extremely narrow with a few small windows. A very thin wall separates the two adjacent rooms. During winters a very large family has to live cramped within two such rooms. I get depressed even to think of the way they live in the cold. They make a big fire indoors around which they dry the damp clothes of their children. When there is continuous rain or snow they cannot go out. Fire from the fireplace and their damp clothes make the air within the rooms very unhealthy;

yet they have to inhale that for hours. The farmer who stays in such a hut earns about rupees thirty a month. He has to pay an annual rent of rupees forty or fifty for his hut, and provide food and clothes for his four or five children and his wife. Yet, this small hut is very clean with all its objects neatly arranged. The iron fireplace is strongly built. At least one of the rooms has an old 'carpet'. Some houses use decorative wallpapers and hang a few pictures on the walls. There are some well-polished wooden cots and a table. On one of the shelves is the Bible. Sometimes they also have other religious books, fictions or even books on farming. Actually, these huts of the poor Englishmen are better furnished, whether necessary or not, than many middleclass homes of our country. Unlike the houses of Indian farmers, these houses do not have any broken doors or windowpanes, foul smelling drains, heaps of cow-dung, or other dirty things scattered in the vicinity. If you visit the house of a British farmer at about nine or ten in the morning, you will find the mistress of the house already extremely tired after her hard work, still she does not shirk from her chores. She will bathe her small children and dress them up in clothes that she herself has washed with care. After that she will feed them, send the elder ones to the nearby school and put the younger ones to sleep. Then she will concentrate on her household chores. Again in the evening, around six or seven o'clock, you will see that the master of the house has returned from his day's hard work. He then takes his evening bread and tea with his family. Later, he relaxes on one of the cots and his wife and children sit near him. The wife does needlework while talking to her husband and the children either listen to their parents' conversation or play among themselves. Though they are not well educated, I feel both pleased and amazed at the discipline that they practice in their everyday life. It is almost impossible to find such neat and well-maintained cottages belonging to our farmers.

The villages here are bigger than those in India. Many of them have a population of about five to six hundred people. The condition of the houses and roads in these villages are better than those in India. In every village there is a small and tidy inn where a person can spend a few days comfortably. We come across many concrete buildings here. Even the houses belonging to carpenters, blacksmiths and other such workers are made of bricks with roofs of red tiles. These houses with gardens in the front and back are much better than the huts of the farmers. They own a greater variety of things compared to the farmers and those are more expensive too. Everything is clean and neatly arranged. But the sad part is that, like the city dwellers, the villagers too are very fond of food and drink. They blow up their money on meat and alcohol.

The agricultural setting in England is starkly different from that in our country. In India, the farmers take land on lease from the landlords and then cultivate. But here, there is a class of people who buy a large portion of land from the big landlords and then employ farm workers for a fixed salary. These people are called the 'farmers' and the land occupied by them is known as 'farm'. There are many kinds of farms here, some grow crops, some keep dairy animals producing milk and milk products and still others keep hens, sheep, horses and other such animals. The farms are very clean and they work in a systematic and disciplined way. Some farmers are in charge of about hundred acres of land for which they have to pay a duty to the land-owner and a 'tax' to the government. Some even take a lease of about four hundred acres of land and cultivate them. The farm labourers work only during the day. They get a salary for it but have no rights over the land. It is the farmers who take care of the field and enjoy the profit from its produce. They live in splendid houses which have a portico in the front and are surrounded by beautiful gardens and huge trees. The interior of the house is beautifully decorated and nicely furnished. Most of the farmers live very lavishly like the rich business men. They are quite educated and intelligent and their wives are also equally intelligent and efficient in domestic chores. In the farms, there are separate spaces for cows, horses, sheep, hens, etc. and these are clean and well ventilated. Almost all the farms have big shelters where horses, cows and other animals are kept under proper care. In some of the farms, these animals are kept in the shelters for about six months at a stretch and fed nutritious food. Almost all the domestic animals of England are bigger and healthier than those in our country. Abundance of fodder, proper care and fresh air make them strong, stout and huge in size. Here the sheep are so big and furry, that an Indian at first sight cannot recognise them as sheep. The cows here are bigger than those found in the hilly regions of our country and produce about ten to twelve litres of milk every day. The most commonly visible horses in and around

London are bigger and healthier than even those belonging to the rich men of our country. Some of the horses here are so huge that they seem to belong to the family of elephants. The horses that are found in and around London are about seven and half to nine feet tall. They are so huge that their Indian counterparts appear no more than babies in comparison. Here they take very good care of the farm animals. Horses here are of a superior breed than those found in other countries; added to it, the British are devoted towards the health of their cattle. Horse races and animal fairs are organised quite frequently here. This too prompts the British to take greater care of their animals in a scientific way.

Here, majority of the farming is carried out by machines instead of human beings, cows or horses. Activities like ploughing, harrowing, threshing or weeding are all done by machines in a faster and better way. Use of these machines has reduced man's hardships considerably. It also saves a lot of time. And taking all expenses into consideration, it is cheaper than farming manually. Sadly, our farmers are ignorant about these machines and our landlords are least bothered about these. Even if they are aware of these, they do not have the urge to change the age-old system of farming. A job that requires a month in India takes about ten days here. As with every other task, the British take an active interest in agriculture too and constantly try to improve their skills. It is their constant endeavour to improvise in this field of knowledge as well. The study of agriculture too requires scientific knowledge, intelligence and experience like every other branch of study. Since land here is not as fertile as that in India nothing can be grown here without much effort. Had the British farmers not used innovative machines and methods of farming to make their soil worth cultivating, nothing probably would have grown here.

Though the farmers and the farm workers appear quite happy from a distance, the condition of the poor is deteriorating day by day in this country. I had said earlier, the cultivators do not have any right over the land; they only toil like labourers here. In spite of earning well, they do not have enough money for a comfortable living due to their extremely extravagant nature. Though the Indian farm workers do not work or earn as much as the British, they are much happier. For them alcohol and meat are not the most indispensable part of life. Hence they do not lead the beastly life of a British farm worker. In England, there is an overall rise in pretension. Even the farm workers spend all their money on fresh meat, bottled liquor and various other luxuries that appeal to their senses. Also there is a constant rise in the number of big farmlands. The farmers are buying up parts of the commons and putting a fence around them. So gradually these commons are either reducing in size or vanishing completely. The farm labourers are therefore not left with any means of keeping their chickens or pigs etc. In this way, since they do not have any right over the land, physical labour is the only option left for earning their daily bread. At times, even their wives and children have to work in the fields in order to earn. Since agriculture is moving in the same direction as industry, farm labourers are reflecting miseries and problems similar to those found among the industrial workers.

Most of the land here is owned by the aristocrats such as the duke, the earl, etc. They distribute and lease out land among the farmers. But these land owners are not like the zamindars of India, especially, the zamindars of Bengal, who are only tax collectors for the British government. The landowners here are quite rich and they donate money for a number of just causes. They are also more educated, progressive and industrious than those in our country. Since only the eldest son inherits the property in England, their properties do not get divided as in our country. Rather, instead of reducing in size, their property increases with time. The darker side of this system is that land here is owned by a handful of people who are only concerned about their own interests. Though they engage in charity, they are not sufficiently well disposed towards the poor people. This can be easily understood by looking at the class distinction and the condition of the poor in this country. The landlords stay in London only for three to four months in the summers and spend rest of the year in their own places, in the palatial houses, surrounded by big gardens.

There are quite a number of prosperous cities of various sizes in England among which Liverpool and Manchester are known to most of the Indians. Cotton imported from various countries reach Liverpool first and from there sent to Manchester where garments are made. Those garments then come back to Liverpool and from the port there, exported to various parts of the world. Nowadays, any ordinary cloth or the *gamchha*, the cloth that Indians use to dry themselves, has the stamp of Manchester on it. Hence almost everyone knows about Manchester cotton. Manchester can easily be called an industrial town. There are huge factories set up in all parts of the town. The machines run throughout the day making various kinds of sounds. I have heard that there is no country in this world where the thread or cloth made in Manchester is not available.

Liverpool is a very big city. It has an approximate population of six lakhs and resembles London in many ways. It is situated in the north of England, close to the sea, on the bank of the river Mersey. It has a number of huge docks which are surrounded by numerous godowns for storing cotton, resembling the walls of a fortress. It seems that entire cotton of the world is brought here. About six miles of Mersey River is crowded with ships. During winters, hundreds of masts of these ships waiting in the harbour make the place look like a dense forest. These ships bring various kinds of merchandise and wealth from different parts of the world. A look at those makes one feel that all the wealth in this world had been created just for England. This city is famous for its trade and commerce; that is what has made it prosperous as well. Most of the places here are as big and rich as London. All the large cities of England show a great love for alcohol but Liverpool is said to be the place in which the most heinous and shameful incidents take place due to alcoholism. It has been my observation in England that the cities which are prosperous due to industries, trade and commerce, suffer more from alcoholism.

I had mentioned elsewhere that this country is famous for peat coal and iron mines. From Buckingham to

Wolverhampton, in the north of England, about twelve miles stretch of land is full of coal mines and iron factories. Smoke and coal make this part of England always appear black. Therefore the British call it 'black country'. This world does not have a place more astonishing. A glance towards this 'black country' or reading about this is enough to make one realise how hard working and tolerant a British person is. It also tells the reason behind England's prosperity. Just as the cities of Manchester and Liverpool are full of cotton mills, cotton godowns, hordes of clothes and many other things, this place is covered in coal and iron—two most useful things for mankind. Since England has prospered a lot due to coal and iron, these two are also known as 'black gold'.

Both the ground beneath and the sky overhead is black in this 'black country'. For many miles underground there are deep mines with various layers formed due to digging. It is difficult to even imagine such a thing. And to see them is an experience so amazing that it cannot be put into words. If you revisit this place at night, it appears quite frightening at first. At night, bright flames leap out of huge furnaces in the iron factories resembling a volcanic eruption. Their noise can be heard from a great distance. Flames emitted by those hundreds of chimneys shoot upwards through the dark sky and look like red feathers of a dancing peacock. Looking at the heaps of burning hot iron it seems that the world is about to end in a great fire. A dense cloud of smoke looks brighter due to the burning furnace beneath it.

Those bright masses of smoke gather together and float above us like clouds. At the same time the sound of blowing wind, clatter of machines, din from the blast furnaces and the loud noise coming from this huge iron hammer numbs both our vision and hearing. One feels like running away from this *patalpuri*. If you go near this place in the morning you can hear the similar sounds but you will not find that terrifying vision of the night. It is hard to believe that such appalling activities are the basis of British prosperity and that these are the most important constituents of British trade and commerce. We understand the great influence of coal and iron in our life only after coming here. Though this place does not seem fit enough for human habitation miners, blacksmiths and other such people have to stay here only. Sun's rays or moonbeams almost never peep into their huts and it is very difficult to understand how they continue with their lives in such a place that has no scope for beauty or relaxation.

Like many aspects of England, its climate is fascinating as well. England is known to have a cold climate but unless one lives here, one cannot understand properly how dynamic it actually is. This place experiences various types of seasons and it is difficult to predict the time for winter to be over or spring's beginning or the span of summer season. Since this is an island, sea breeze blowing from all sides, prevent the onset of extreme winters or scorching summers as found in France, Germany and other neighbouring countries. Yet, I have not seen such horrible and fluctuating climate anywhere else. Due to the Atlantic Ocean in the west, there is continuous storm and rain coming in from that direction. At times, bitter cold winds blow from the north and the east. Except for two to three months, rest of the year in this place is very difficult for the ailing or weak persons. And if the foreigners visiting this place do not take proper care, they too can easily fall sick. But along with so many evils, there are some positive aspects too. Though the climate is ever-changing it is not unhealthy. Since the British grow up in this extreme type of climate, they turn out to be very tough and do not hesitate to undertake difficult tasks. British sailors, since they are born in such a country, learn to overcome all difficulties and sail on the seas for days and nights, exploring various countries. Such a challenging environment makes the British tough, strong, capable and industrious. It is said that if a person can tolerate this insufferable British climate for a considerable period of time, he can easily live in any country of the world.

In England, the seasons follow the order of summer, autumn, winter and spring. But a few summer days can get as cold as winter while some days in winter can be similar to autumn season. Rain and storm can upset life at any point of time or season of the year. People here always live in the fear of cold and difficult days.

June, July and August are the summer months of this country. During this time, about fifteen to twenty days are as hot as the month of *Ashadh*[xxxiv] in our country. Rest of the year enjoys quite cool weather, similar to *Kartik* or *Agrahayan*[xxxv] in our country. During this period nights are very short. Within twenty-four hours, it is night only from four o'clock to eight o'clock and towards the end of June, there is light in the sky throughout the night. For an Indian, it is surprising to see evening setting in around nine or ten o'clock and the day break by one or two o'clock. But it does not remain so for long. Gradually, as the duration of day decreases, our amazement also subsides. In England, summer is the season of happiness. During these months, trees grow fresh leaves, flowers and fruits and make the villages, cities and towns of England look beautiful. Everybody enjoys this period of the year. Many people who work as hard as a donkey through the year take rest during this time.

September, October and November are the autumn months here. But it is very different from the season of *sharat*[xxxvi] in our country. Nature loses splendour and turns depressing towards the end of autumn. Trees look dismal without any leaves and flowers. Heaps of dried leaves can be found beneath each tree and every gush of air sheds more leaves. Such drastic changes within a span of these three months perturb us. Day breaks at seven, its duration reduced and evening sets in by five or six o' clock. Cities once again put on their sombre look and prepare themselves to embrace the harsh winter. People leave their summer amusements and concentrate on their own jobs. Those who come to visit England now return to their respective homes. November is a terrible month as there is dense fog. It marks the beginning of English winter. December, January and February are the actual winter months. This is a difficult period as nature is extremely hostile: severe cold, dense fog, occasional drizzling and snowfall—all these together make human life thoroughly miserable. Often, in January and February, almost everything freezes—roads freeze and become as hard as stone and at times water kept in earthen pitchers freeze causing the pitchers to crack. A great crisis of water ensues. Water that is there in the house freezes into ice and has to be melted for use again. Sometimes water freezes in the underground pipelines that supply water and cut off domestic water supply. Some winters are so severe that the even man-made water tanks in the gardens freeze. The British entertain themselves in various ways even in such freezing climate. When the roads, fields and the entire neighbourhood is covered in snow and turn both hard and slippery, young men put on their skating shoes and glide around in a serpentine motion. Some of them rush down in high speed through these snow covered roads in a kind of a vehicle that has no wheels. On some nights, there is a lot of revelry here. Men, women, girls and boys, carrying their torches, happily go for walks together to some frozen lakes or canals. Their laughter and voices can be heard from a long distance. Every year winter is not equally severe here. Had it been so, the British would have found it very difficult to survive. I do not need to mention that it is impossible to live in a house without a fireplace here. While going out, people need to wear layers of warm clothing to keep their limbs from getting numb in the freezing cold outside. In some parts of England winter is so severe that if people sit outdoors, parts of their body or the entire body might get frozen. Winter days are extremely short; mornings begin around eight or nine o'clock. And by three or four o'clock, evening sets in. Days are mostly cloudy. The sun either remains invisible, or even if it is visible, it appears so cold and dull that it is as good as not being there. During winter here, you need to burn a lot of oil and wood and also need warm clothes. At times when the entire surrounding is frozen, the labourers have to stop their work. Therefore in this season the poor people suffer a lot. March, April and May are months of spring. March, which is the spring season here, is actually colder than *magh*[xxxvii] in India. Throughout March a strong wind blows. In spite of all the layers of our clothing cold wind penetrates our skin and rattles our bones. These are at times accompanied with rain and snow. By April the severity of winter reduces. Yet even then the temperature remains similar to or lower than that of Indian winters. There is incessant rainfall in April, similar to the rainy season of India. Farmers start cultivation in this period. New plants grow. Days become longer and the nights, shorter. Sun gets bigger and brighter. England seems to get a new lease of life. May is the actual month of spring here. This is the time when the entire flora looks fresher, decked up in green leaves and flowers of various colours. The towns and villages look brighter. Entire vegetation, from huge trees to small grasses, is beautifully adorned with flowers in bloom. Whether you visit a garden or a field, a town or countryside, everywhere you will find an abundance of flowers. But sadly, such lovely flowers exist only for a couple of months. In the months of May and June, a pleasant breeze blows and the sun is soothing. Every country has its share of happiness and sorrow. Here too the people suffer a lot in winters, but they forget all that when they enjoy a pleasant summer.

EDUCATION AND EDUCATION SYSTEM

The education system of a country helps us to understand how cultured and progressive that country is. Prevalence of higher education, education among the masses, literacy rate among the poor and how much of the education is converted into practical use are some of the factors that help us to decide how prosperous and civilized a country is. Let us take the example of China. Though in terms of its education system it is much better than most of the Asian countries—majority of its common people can read and write, and it has a rigorous examination system, yet it lags far behind the European countries in terms of progress. The reason behind it is that the quality of higher education in China is not as good as in the European countries and though they have some scientific knowledge, they have not yet learnt its application. Now look at the Germans. They are extremely well-educated; even a layman knows two to three languages and is proficient in all aspects of general awareness. Their scholars are famous throughout the world, making new inventions or solving difficult mysteries. Still, England is more prosperous than Germany. Unlike the British, Germans have not learnt to make use of their knowledge. The English say that, though German scientists make new inventions it is the English who enjoy their benefits.

None of the towns in England lack in educational facilities. Even the villages have two to three schools. So neither a city dweller nor a village folk, wants to remain uneducated. It is impossible to count the number of schools and colleges that England has. Apart from these there are many other means of mass education as well. Anyone in pursuit of education is bound to be delighted by the educational set up here. Here the people do not wait for any government aid to set up a school or college. Most of such institutions are founded by a common man or a rich person. Also, just as there are schools for boys, there are ample schools for girls as well. Wherever you go, you will find an almost equal number of schools for boys and girls. Apart from that, in many places, particularly London, women study alongside men in the top colleges.

Along with studies, the British are skilled in physical activities as well which makes their body stronger. Most of the schools have provision for sports like gymnastics, wrestling and cricket. They start going to school at the age of six or seven and continue their education either in schools or colleges till they reach the age of twenty five or twenty six. But their actual education is not limited to schools. Once they complete their schools their process of self-learning starts. That is the time when they are actually educated. In our country, it is only in Bengal that education is so widely respected as well as practiced. That is why the people of Bengal have progressed more as compared to the rest of the country. Unfortunately, most of our young people stop learning as soon as they finish their college because they consider their education to end there. But here, people consider college education and the related examinations to be just a signpost towards the actual storehouse of knowledge. In their educational institutions, they only learn the right way to gain knowledge. Later, with their own efforts they enrich their minds with knowledge from various fields. While in school, they study a limited number of books which keep their knowledge confined, their only motive being how to compete with their classmates. This makes the students enthusiastic about studies. But once they complete their college education, they develop a yearning for the vast resource of knowledge. That is the real source of education. Taking this as their capital, they delve into the vast reservoir of knowledge and develop themselves.

There are a number of people here who spend their entire life in educational pursuits. For some of them, writing new books is like a game, some enjoy discovering new celestial objects, and there are some others who have chosen various disciplines of Science as their area. There are numerous poets and authors and also many mathematicians, astronomers and scientists from various other disciplines. Here the schools, colleges, clubs, hospitals and clinics are run by well qualified people. Many people here work in important posts like that of barristers, attorney, doctor, teachers, etc. Though England is a prosperous country, many educated people here fall prey to poverty. The reason behind this is excess of education. With the rise in the number of educated people, there is a proportionate increase in the competition among them in all aspects. Here, a number of university educated people have to wander in search of jobs. There are no vacancies for a teaching post; if there comes up an advertisement for a single teaching post, more than five hundred people apply for it. If any teacher dies, more than three hundred people nurture a dream of getting that job. With the development in education, the number of educated people is also increasing in this country. So it is very difficult to find jobs for all of them.

In our country, Hemchandrababu[xxxviii], Bankimbabu[xxxix] and a few such authors have created some great literary works and have made Bengal proud. That is why they are famous throughout Bengal. But here there are so many authors of similar repute that their names are not that well-known as well. People do not value things that they have in abundance. Yet in England, the importance of education is not less than that in any other country. Though the British are slaves of wealth, they do not ignore education. That is why they have already established many schools and are still doing so. Due to their love for education hundreds of books are being written and published on various subjects and lakhs of people read them. This shows the extent of influence that education has in their society and the pride they take in it. English language is so rich because the British respect education. There is neither any subject in the world nor any new invention on which the British have not written a book. A visit to the libraries is enough to understand the range of English literature. There are twenty to twenty five thousand books stacked in the rooms. Apart from that there are many more books that are either being printed or are about to be. There is no dearth of books on complex and difficult subjects such as geography, history, science, philosophy, etc. And again there are plenty of books like biographies, dramas, farces and novels which are thrilling and entertaining. There are about hundred such libraries in England. I have already talked about the British Museum Library; apart from that there are a number of other libraries in London itself whose collection go up to forty to fifty thousand or even a lakh.

Though a number of people here know foreign languages such as French, German, etc. they do not like to read books written in any language other than English. If there is any book par excellence published in any foreign language, they immediately translate it into their own. On the contrary, these days many English educated Indians do not enjoy reading books in their mother tongue. Some even hate doing so. Perhaps lack of good books is the reason behind this. But instead of being contemptuous, if they could write some important and useful books in their own languages or even translate some good works from other languages, they could serve their own language and people better. There are very few people who can access knowledge from foreign texts. If there are no good books available in the language of the common people, we cannot expect them to progress or be benefitted in any way.

You can find plenty of books, newspapers, magazines, etc. in this country which signifies the number of educated people here. The common people here, whether men or women, are educated enough to read and understand newspapers, plays or novels easily. Almost every British has an interest in government and politics and that is why they consider reading newspapers to be an important duty. In our country, certain section of the society, say the shopkeepers—

grocers, butchers, green grocers etc., do not even know what a newspaper is. But in this country, people belonging to these sectors too, take a lot of interest in reading newspapers and gain knowledge from them. Even the coachmen travelling to various places eagerly read newspapers to know what is happening both within the country and abroad, or to remain updated about wars going on in any part of the world, etc. They are not just passive readers; rather, they critically analyse and hold animated exchanges among themselves on various political, social and other issues. In India and a few other countries people believe that only those in the government must agitate about all these issues and rest of the people need not lose their sleep over these. But no one thinks or talks like this here. The people here believe that every individual has a say in the country's governance, however small that might be. Therefore it is the duty of each one to critically consider the pros and cons of their government's actions even if there are a number of people selected for this job.

A mere carpenter in England can tell you more about the government and other issues of the country than even a well-educated clerk in India. Reading newspaper is almost an integral part of their daily breakfast here. If you visit any of the houses in the morning, you will find people taking food and reading newspapers simultaneously, fulfilling both their physical hunger and intellectual cravings. While visiting a shop we find the shopkeeper reading newspapers during his free hours; his face reflects various emotions of happiness or sorrow according to the news item which he is reading. Even the maid servant here reads newspaper in her leisure hours to improve her knowledge, after completing the day's work. In this country, there are a vast number of newspapers and they are available at an extremely low rate. So even the poor people can spend a few pennies to procure and read them.

In London, at least twenty different newspapers are published each morning. 'Times' is the most important one and it costs about two *annas*. Other important newspapers are 'Daily News', 'Daily Telegraph', Standard' and 'Chronicle'. Each of them costs only 3 paisa and they are the ones which are generally read by the common people. There are seven to eight evening newspapers, two of them cost one and a half paisa only and the rest are priced around 3 paisa. Some excellent dailies and weeklies are published from other cities too. One can find a couple of newspapers even in the smallest cities of England.

Previously, people belonging to the lower classes or the extremely poor ones did not have access to education. But a few years back a law was passed which made it compulsory for every parent to send each child to school. If they fail to do so, they will be fined and their children will be taken away by some school. Government has established a number of schools for the poor children. They are called 'board schools' where these children can be educated either free of cost or for a very little money. The country has benefitted greatly by this law. Ten years ago some people were completely deprived of education but now even those belonging to the lowest of classes can at least read and write. Perhaps fifty years hence there will not be a single uneducated person in England.

There are some famous and old schools here called the 'public schools'. These are mostly attended by the children of rich families and a few from the middle classes. The chief among these are 'Harrow', 'Eton' and 'Rugby'. Along with studies, here the students are also trained in games and physical exercises. They excel in various kinds of sports such as 'cricket', 'football', 'tennis' and rowing. Harrow and Eton constantly compete against each other. Both the schools try hard to remain unbeaten in all fields because whichever side loses, the students of that school feel greatly insulted. The students of both the schools form into various societies and organise debate competitions. Their competitive attitude helps them to stand out both in studies and games. Since both schools maintain an equivalent standard, such endeavours only improve their qualities. Sports such as rowing and cricket are organised among the students of both the schools. The one who wins is rewarded. So the students take a lot of care in their education.

If we compare the level of education between England and India, only Bengalis among all the Indian races can be compared to the British. But in spite of being intelligent and clever, the Bengalis generally lack physical and mental alacrity by lacking in health. Bengalis in their seventeenth or eighteenth year consider themselves to have crossed almost half of their youth. Thus they maintain a serious appearance, abstain from all kinds of physical games and activities which help in the development of physical strength and consider those to be mere child's play. Many of our countrymen believe that if they undertake such activities, they will lose their focus from studies or become wayward. I do not have much to tell them, they should once come and see how games and academics coexist in the schools and colleges of England; only then they shall get rid of all their misconceptions. I think everyone will agree that education of the mind is closely associated with physical well being and vigour. Biographies of great and learned people tell us that many of them who belonged to the poor families had indulged in various physical games in their childhood. These activities had made them strong and healthy and also helped them in their later lives in their pursuit of education.

Everybody knows that if we are not physically fit, we do not feel mentally fit too; when we suffer from some mental agony we feel a physical weakness as well. When the body is healthy and strong, the mind is fresh and able. So it is not surprising that the healthy boys will be better in studies and retain their knowledge for a longer period. One must keep in mind that human beings have both mind and body. Taking care of one and neglecting the other would eventually harm us. With physical weakness, lack of spirit, fear and many such vices set in. I had heard about some young Indian men who had earned university degrees with distinction quite early in life. But as they neglected their physical well-being and exercised their minds day and night they fell sick and lost their lives quite early. Is not that very sad? The British understand such things well. They might neglect education of their mind but never their body. In a number of places in this country, children indulge in physical exercises and games, neglecting their studies. They acquire better skill in these activities than in education. Though too much of everything is bad, it is much better to live long with a healthy body than to lose all physical and mental well being at an early stage.

Just as the big public schools here have excellent arrangements for both studies and sports, Harrow and Eton, the two important schools for the rich ones here have an evil tradition as well. This tradition is called 'fagging'[xl]. The younger and weaker boys have to serve as slaves or servants to the bigger and stronger boys. Each of the elder boys has a number of such servants. They obey their orders, clean their rooms, dust the lamp stands, toast their bread, help them at their play, wake them up in the morning, and do many such chores which are otherwise done by servants. Nowadays there has been a drop in this evil practice and hopefully it will be soon completely eradicated. Teachers here are not very strict with their students. So from an early age the students learn self-help and self- respect. The chief motive of these schools is to teach the students Greek and Latin and to help them compose beautiful pieces of prose and poetry in these languages. But nowadays they have also included arithmetic and science in their curricula. I have heard that one has to spend about two hundred rupees per month in order to study at Harrow and Eton.

In England higher education is provided only by the universities. There are eleven universities in Great Britain and Ireland together. The chief among them are Oxford, Cambridge, London and Dublin. London University was established in 1838, towards the beginning of Queen Victoria's rule. It is not as expensive as the Oxford or the

Cambridge and it does not have any kind of orthodoxy, religious or otherwise. Irrespective of their race or religion, people can pursue their education here without any hassle. It is more economical too. The system of these universities is quite similar to that of the University of Calcutta. The only difference is that the examinations here are much tougher than those in Calcutta. The universities in Calcutta, Bombay and Madras have been established along the lines of the University of London. As they are exactly like the London University there's no need to describe this university in a great detail. London University is different from the rest in one particular matter. Here women too can pursue education in the same way as men. It is comparatively more famous because it was the first university to award degrees to women. Oxford and Cambridge have followed London University to a certain extent in this matter. In these two universities, women can take up certain examinations like men but they cannot obtain degrees such as B.A or M.A. like the latter. Some new colleges for women have been established under the universities of Oxford and Cambridge recently but the University of London remains the chief centre of higher education for British women. Its doors are open to all irrespective of their gender. It is wonderful to find both men and women attending the same college and same lessons under the same teachers and attaining same degrees after qualifying in the same examinations. When both breathe in the same air, eat the same food and live in the same house, then who will not like to see both of their minds to be nourished in the same way? Oxford and Cambridge

Universities are almost similar to each other. Both are extremely rich and ancient. In certain matters they differ completely from all the other universities of the world. Oxford University had been established in 886 A.D. by King Alfred. People say that Cambridge University is even older. In this book I am going to provide details of the Cambridge University in particular and all my readers can also know about the Oxford University from it. The important goals of these universities are to provide education, take examinations, confer degrees, and distribute scholarships and prizes to students. Apart from the college faculty members, there is another set of teachers here. They give 'lectures' in the university which can be attended by the students of all the colleges. Cambridge offers various courses, prime among them being mathematics, Latin, Greek and Natural Sciences. Its mathematics is famous throughout the world. Prizes and scholarships are impartially awarded to those students of these departments who show overall excellence. These awards are given from the money donated by various individuals. This university also has excellent libraries, museum, botanical garden, etc. Those who are responsible for maintaining discipline among the students are known as 'proctors'. These proctors and their assistants are like the police in the university. They keep vigil and if the students commit any offence, they punish them as well.

This university holds different exams for different subjects. One can earn a degree by qualifying in any one of these. Every student has to qualify a 'previous' examination before taking up the final examination to earn the degree.

This examination is commonly known as the 'little go'. Here two kinds of degrees are conferred—general and honours. The examination for an honours degree is comparatively more difficult. Almost all the universities of this country, such as London University and others follow this system. In Calcutta, we do not have such different degrees. In Cambridge University, the examination for Honours degree is known as 'tripos'. A person gets a B.A. degree on qualifying any of the degree offering examination. Perhaps many of us are not aware that in this university, one does not have to appear for another examination in order to obtain the M.A. degree. Those who procure B.A. degree can get the M.A. degree after three more years. Cambridge has seventeen colleges under it. These have been established at various points of time by grants given by various great people. Each college has a principal who is generally called 'master'. He and some other people with the title of 'fellow' run the college. The fellows select the principal of the college. They get a yearly stipend out of the money provided by the founder of the college. The number of fellows differs in every college. Some colleges have only seven to eight fellows while in some there are as many as twenty to twenty-five. If there is a vacancy for fellowship, the principal and other fellows of that college select the best person from among those who have attained the degree from that college and appoint him to that post. The fellow in charge of studies and other related things of the students is known as a 'tutor'. The students can ask their questions and learn from him. He is like an advisor and guardian to the students. The fellow who is in charge of religious matters pertaining to students is known as 'dean'. Each college has a small church. It is the dean's responsibility to see that the students attend its services regularly. His role is that of the priest. Each college has different teachers to teach various subjects to the students. Often the fellows of the college act as teachers. The best students of the colleges get scholarships. These scholarships range from thirty rupees a month to about two hundred.

The students either live within the college premises or in some of the assigned houses in the city. They have to attend the college cathedral once a day regularly, either in the morning or in the evening. But nowadays this rule has slackened quite a bit in a number of colleges. The college authorities exempt students from this rule if there is some special reason for it. In every college the students are taught from nine o'clock in the morning to twelve noon. In the evening, every one dines in the 'hall'. The students sit on one side and the administrators on the other. Before and after dining, one of the students says the 'grace'. Most of the students indulge in outdoor exercises or physical activities in the evening. They take a lot of interest in rowing boats, playing cricket and other such pursuits. Sometimes, they end up taking more interest in these than in their studies. Each college has separate societies for debating, rowing, cricket, etc. Also, there is a *milansamaj* that is social group to help students interact among themselves. This is similar to a 'club', and one can also read newspapers or other books here. The students meet here once a week to discuss and debate upon political, social and other issues. The kind of confidence and interest they show during these discussions will make one feel that these are mini parliaments. Apart from this, Cambridge also has other associations for people interested in literature, music, etc. In order to graduate, one has to study in a college for three years and then pass an examination conducted by the University. Some people take up the examination without going to the college. Such students spend much less for their education but they remain completely shut out from the pleasures of the college life. Here the students wear gown and a flat hat when they go somewhere, or attend their lectures, go to the church, dine in the hall or take their degrees. Perhaps after reading this description of the universities, people will realise that getting a degree from here is a costly affair. One has to spend about three hundred rupees per month. Some spend even more but some of them manage with much less as well. Generally, boys from affluent families come to these universities. So one ends up spending more in order to keep up with them. But studying at Oxford or Cambridge has its own advantages as well. Since the students live in the same house, eat together and attend the same lectures, they develop a strong friendship among themselves. Since every college and university has various clubs and societies, students get better opportunities for interacting among themselves. They also play and exercise together. Also, the fact that they all are young and come from similar background, helps them to bond easily. Often these friendships remain strong lifelong. The students get a glimpse of the worldly life here and gain experience regarding people and their characters, lifestyle, etc.

THE BRITISH RELIGION AND RELIGIOUS FESTIVALS

Before coming to England I used to think that, everyone here follows the same religious tradition. But once here, I was much surprised to find the variations that existed within a single religion. There is no want of religious variety in our country where people practicing different faith, such as the Hindus, Muslims, Christians, etc. live together. Within Hinduism itself, there are so many different sects that it is almost impossible to count all of them. It is not surprising that a vast country like India would have many different religions and religious groups, but England is a much smaller country where majority of the population practice Christianity. A very small section of the population practice Judaism or other religions. Yet you can find more than one hundred and twenty-five different cults among the Christians here.

Christianity is divided into two main branches—the Roman Catholics and the Protestants. Majority of the British people are Protestant Christians and Protestantism has a number of different factions. Bible is the primary religious text for all these sects but each of them focuses on certain aspects of it, overlooking others. They have widely divergent religious practices. They believe Jesus Christ to be the Son of God and the Saviour of man. They say that Christ had taken birth to salvage the sinners. Nowadays a few communities consider Jesus Christ to be a mere human being. They believe that he was an extremely saintly and religious person who guided the people to the right path; yet these communities too acknowledge themselves as Christians.

The main Protestant Church is known as the Church of England. A little more than half the entire British population belongs to this church. This has become the national religion because it has the patronage and supervision of the national government. The Church of England has two archbishops, about twenty eight bishops and their subordinates to carry out its work. People treat them at par with the noble men and they attend the House of Lords in the parliament to look after the affairs related to the government. All of them are very well-paid. The two bishops receive fifteen thousand and ten thousand rupees respectively per month. Other priests also get somewhere between two thousand four hundred and ten thousand rupees.

Bishops are supreme among the ecclesiastical community. They are helped by a few assistant bishops who in turn have priests subordinate to them. These priests do not earn any fixed salary. They are given a parish which becomes the means to their livelihood. All of them do not earn the same. Some may earn about a thousand a month from their parish but majority of them earn much less. A few of them earn as less as a hundred rupees a month. These parishes are owned by the rich people like the duke, earl and other members of the aristocracy. They dole out these parishes as gift to whoever they want.

In this country, the ecclesiastical profession is considered to be quite profitable and of great dignity. Just as people take training to be doctors and barristers, many of them take training for ecclesiastical jobs as well. Quite often sons of the aristocratic families happily join the orders and daughters of such families prefer to marry the priests. Almost every cleric belongs to a noble family and is educated. They hold degrees from the universities of Oxford or Cambridge. Many among them are wealthy as well. Some of the clergy lead a prosperous lifestyle; they maintain nice carriages and horses and keep to the rich and the powerful. The common people revere them. In the country sides, the parsons visit the houses of their parishioners. They affectionately enquire after the education of the children and chastise them in case of any wrong doings. They preach against consumption of alcohol, talk to the people about their jobs and advice them on various issues. Though there are a few among the clergy who are very orthodox or love to lead a life of luxury, they are generally pious and honest. Under their care the common people have developed quite a lot in terms of education and morality.

Here, I do not want to engage in a comparative discussion of the merits of our religions. Almost every religion has its faith in God and most of them talk about piety and sin. It is not that only the Hindus are superstitious, even the Christians are. If we weed out the undesirable parts of both the religions, it becomes difficult to judge which among them is better. Hinduism has degraded a lot. While the Hindus themselves have been reduced to almost insignificance the Christians have progressed much. Their influence has spread throughout the world. Therefore it is not surprising that many people will consider Christianity to be the best religion in this world. British consider Christianity to be supreme and the only way to man's salvation. Even if any other religion appears to be better and free from superstitions, no British person, whether educated or not, will convert to that religion and insult that of his own. This proves that whether an Englishman is pious by nature or not, his faith in his religion is unshakable. Their self-esteem is probably the cause behind this. Our own educated Pandita Ramabai[xli] on coming to England has denounced Hinduism and embraced Christianity, much to the chagrin of all the Hindus. Such degradation of self respect cannot find a parallel among the Englishmen.

The British appear quite religious by nature. Instead of leaving the religious duties to be performed by the priests only, they actively participate in them. Going to church every Sunday with the entire family and reading Bible or discussing religious matters at home are some of the very important engagements of the British people. One can also find a lot of religious orthodoxy here as well. It is almost a sacrilege if someone works on a Sunday or does not visit the church. Playing cards or reading novels, etc. on a Sunday is considered almost a sacrilege. I have already discussed how London appears on a Sunday; it is similar in all other parts of England as well. I have heard that at a few places, one is not even supposed to talk loudly on a Sunday.

One can see both orthodoxy as well as hypocrisy here. Some people visit churches for the sake of appearances. Most of the young women go there to show off their attire. A number of people do not understand the true significance of religion, nor do they want to understand. Many young people of London do not have much faith in religion. Like the newly emerging class in our society, even here there are some who do not care much for any religion or are completely atheists. Then there are some other people who believe in monotheism and consider Christ to be a human being. They are very few in number. In London there are only two Unitarian churches. I had visited one of those on a Sunday. I felt as if I was sitting at the Brahmo Samaj. The only difference was that here the prayer was said in English.

England has numerous churches of various sizes and communities. However, one cannot see the poor frequenting to any of these. In almost all the countries majority of the poor practice some religion. But here, they not only lack virtues like kindness or compassion, they are ignorant of religious practices as well. They are just Christian by name. Nowadays, a new society called the 'Salvation army' has been formed to try and inculcate religious feelings among the poor. Like the *sankirtans*[xlii] of our country, they sing religious songs on the roads. Their songs which have tunes similar to those of our *tappa*[xliii] or *panchali*[xliv] are meant to draw the attention of the poor people. Their prayers involve various physical actions or poses. It is true that they have rescued many drunkards and sinners from their chosen path of evil, but they have also irked some people by presenting religion as a form of entertainment.

The number of Christian festivals is much lesser than that of the Hindus. In our country the true Hindus pray and worship at every available occasion but it is very rare to find the English praying on a day apart from Sundays. We do not reserve any day exclusively for prayers and for enjoyment but the British do not lag behind in their acts of devotion as they reserve one whole day for it. On that day, that is Sunday, they do not indulge in any entertainment activities. Most of us must have heard the names of their important occasions like the Christmas or the Good Friday. Christmas is the greatest of all their festivals.

The British celebrate Christmas on the 25th of December. This day is called Christmas because Jesus Christ was born on this day. I do not know why it is called *Borodin*[xlv] (long day) in our country. One of the reasons can be because it is the most important occasion celebrated in the land of our rulers; or perhaps people lovingly call it so because it has the shortest duration of day time. Though Christmas is said to be a religious occasion, I do not find much correlation between the religion and its celebration. There is no fixed religious activity or ritual associated with the festivity and even praying to Christ is not mandatory. Actually, Christmas in its current form is more of a social or a family occasion. The British follow certain funny set of rules at this time. These have been continuing from the times of the 'Druids' of the ancient ages. In those days these had religious significance but over the years the British have accommodated these as social customs. Just as the Durga Puja in Bengal, Christmas in England is a time for great enjoyment. People indulge in a lot of charities during this time. This festival of happiness brings true delight in the minds of those Englishmen fraught with worry and miseries of life. Many people have to stay away from their friends and families in different parts of the world on account of their livelihood. But on this day they all come together to enjoy each other's company and wish their near and dear ones. Amid such merriment and feasting in the company of friends, the Christian year gradually takes its leave. During this time people think about the year about to end and at the same time feel hopeful about the coming year.

The evening before the Christmas is known as the Christmas Eve and it is as pleasing as the *Sashthi*^{xlvi} of our Durga Puja. On this evening the entire family sits together in a room. In the middle of the room a branch from the Mistletoe tree hangs from the ceiling and a huge log burns brightly in the fireplace. Traditionally, on this day each member of the family, young or old, men or women, kisses each other freely under the mistletoe branch. So everyone gathers under this branch and kisses each other amidst a lot of laughter and fun. This day the generally silent and grave British assume a new appearance. Even the boys and the men of the houses play children's games like the blind man's bluff and others. Later, tired after all the excitement, they sit around the fire for dinner. There are certain dishes kept particularly for this occasion. At the centre of the table there are hot apples boiling in a big bowl. Its flavour and the sweet sound of its boiling makes it irresistible for the people. After getting their fill of many such delicacies and wine, the entire family along with their servants waits around the fire till midnight to welcome Christmas in their homes. During this time they play various games and tell stories. If it coincides with a heavy snowfall or storm well past midnight, some of them narrate spine chilling spooky stories. In between they also drink alcohol and sing songs to welcome Christmas with almost everyone either lending a voice or clapping loudly.

The Hindus, on their religious occasions, keep a fast throughout the day and pray to God. Thereafter they feel happy to invite a large number of people to a feast. But on Christmas here, some people might just visit the church in the morning; and later in the day, all the people, whether rich or poor enjoy a feast. Many people save money to spend on food during Christmas and on this day they treat themselves to a variety of delicacies including meat, wine, fruits and sweets. Their main course includes special dishes like roasted beef, plum pudding, etc, accompanied by alcohol. After meals they engage in music, dance or various games. The sounds of their merriment can often be heard from a long distance.

Just as we wear new clothes during Durga Puja, people here do so on Christmas. They also send various eatables as gifts to their relatives and friends. Apart from these, friends send Christmas cards to each other. These cards look like playing cards with different kinds of floral designs on it. There are verses containing good wishes printed on them. Even if a person has spent the entire year in extreme sorrow, he will spend this day cheerfully with good food, music, laughter and games. And those who cannot afford to eat to their fill or have proper clothes, they wear new clothes and eat to their heart's content on this day; everyone talks of food and enjoyment. But this entertainment remains confined within the family and a few close friends. Actually one can even say that this festival is not related to religion but to food. Very rarely a rich person might distribute food or clothes among the poor here; but unlike India, people here do not have a habit of making large donations to the needy. In our country people generously feed and give clothes to thousands of people during festivals. But here the British benevolence remains confined within their own families and this selfish race finds its happiness in feeding themselves only.

THE BRITISH: AN INDEPENDENT RACE—THEIR GOVERNMENT AND ELECTION OF THE MEMBERS OF THE PARLIAMENT

If someone asks me about the most striking difference between England and India, I shall reply that while England is a free country, India is still under bondage. It is said that even a slave becomes free as soon as he steps on the English soil. Even I can discern some new emotions within me since the time I have started breathing in the free air of independent England and living in the company of these independent people. But I cannot explain these newly emerging feelings to my sisters in India. As long as I was in India, I knew nothing of these. Back then, I could not even imagine that human life could have such different facets. By reading books I knew of countries that were independent, those that were under foreign domination or those that had an autocratic form of government and I used to read about different countries in books and learnt of countries which were independent, which were not, which had an autocratic form of government, etc. and I understood them in my own way then. But I did not know that these had so many underlying layers of meanings and such complexities. Words like dictatorship, autocracy, etc, did not leave any mark on my mind at that time. They were simply words that I came across. But now I realise that I had been blind then. Just as a blind person finds everything dark and she cannot understand the difference between night and day however hard she might try; mine was the vision of an enslaved person. Now I can understand the true meanings of the things that I had read in my childhood. The more I compare the two countries, the more knowledge I gain.

In spite of all the faults that the English might have, they shine with the best of human virtues as well. They do not lag behind anyone in terms of physical strength, spirit, and industriousness. It is because of these virtues that they are such an independent and progressive race. For example, there are many people in some countries who would be content with their bestial state and never raise their head against their tormentors however much they be tortured or repressed. Similarly, in this world there are races, which in spite of being subjugated live their lives in utter compliance. They happily carry on with their usual life, even after surrendering their country to some autocratic ruler or to some foreign power. They have lost all their honour and pride. The English people are totally different from all such races.

Here people do not know autocracy. They have a queen but they are also aware that a country cannot be ruled according to the wishes of a single person. Each of them has some responsibilities towards the governance of the country. They are fully aware that the country belongs to its people. As long as they are alive, they will not tolerate any one person, whether a foreigner or one of their own, trying to rule the country single-handedly. In fact, though many tasks are accomplished in the name of the king or queen, it is the people of England who perform them. Ask a British person about wars, he will answer with a lot of enthusiasm using phrases like "our clever soldiers", or "our brave people", etc. One often comes across spirited phrases like "this independent country" and "I am a British".

In this country nobody tolerates another's domination, or allow anyone else to get the better of him. No one can force his opinion on another. Each one can express his views freely. None is scared of the king or the government. There is complete freedom and nobody can force people to do things against their wishes. Everyday scores of newspapers are published and in these all government actions are critically analysed. People express their independent views unhesitatingly. Any crime or injustice within the country is immediately reported by the newspapers; the issues are generally discussed in every home till they are addressed. Newspapers are like mirrors of public opinion. Common people express themselves through newspapers and the authorities too accept their opinions instead of neglecting them. The reason behind such overwhelming influence of newspapers in this country is the complete freedom enjoyed by the common people here. Another remarkable quality of the British is that they never misuse their freedom. They are alert and thoughtful in all their work. They never act unfairly or unreasonably just because they have the power.

British history consistently provides us with such examples. Even in the ancient times of the Saxons, the wise men participated in the court and advised their king regarding sundry matters. They were also the ones who chose their ruler. After the Normans conquered England, there were some problems in the system of governance, but even then the king had not turned totally despotic. The common people did not enjoy much freedom then but the king was under the control of the nobles. Gradually, these aristocrats had reduced the power of the king quite considerably. Many a times the king depended on their advice. When the Normans and the Saxons intermingled, the nobles of both these races sat together in the court and counselled the king. Kingship became a matter of inheritance. As a matter of practice, down the years, some of the common people also got nominated to the king's council of advisors. In this way that advisory body took the form of the modern day parliament. But its roots can be traced back to the ancient times.

In the seventeenth century, King Charles I had tried to establish an autocratic rule but he lost his life in that endeavour. He had tried to levy a number of taxes without consulting the parliament. Though most of his nobles were with him, other members of the parliament could not tolerate the move and protested against the king. The king did not pay heed to them and thus started a battle between the king and the members of the parliament. The king's party was badly defeated and the king was beheaded. This increased the common people's say in the government and ended the monopoly of the aristocrats. Since the eighteenth century, no single party of the parliament could indiscriminately frame and promulgate any law for its benefits. Kingship is hereditary in this country. Just as one inherits property, the crown of England too is inherited by the heir to the throne. Among all the European countries, it is only in England that a woman can rule. In Indian history, many Hindu queens are celebrated for their chastity and spirited achievements, and we are not surprised to hear of a queen's rule. But one does not hear of a woman's rule in countries like France, Germany or Russia.

Parliament is the law-making body in this country. It has two different branches: the House of Lords and the House of Commons. In the House of Lords, members of the aristocratic families and the clergy discuss and debate on issues related to the governance of the country. Two archbishops and twenty-four bishops sit in this house but the number of lords is not fixed. It depends on the wishes of the king or the queen. There are five kinds of titles for them—duke, marquise, earl, viscount and baron. The people, who hold these titles, are customarily called lords. Like kingship, these titles and the power of these title holders are hereditary. The House of Lords is the highest court of justice in the British society. It is this house which sits on the final judgement of any legal issue. The House of Commons has about six hundred and seventy members. The people of the country, except the nobility, choose the representatives of this house. The members of the House of Commons are the elected representatives of the cities, districts, villages or universities and in that capacity they present their views on matters pertaining to the governance. The special power of the House of Commons lies in the fact that they control the financial matters and that is why they can keep a check on the king.

Ministers are appointed from the two houses of the parliament and it is these ministers who actually run the country in the name of their king or queen. Any new bill can be proposed in either of the two houses. When any law is first presented it is called a 'bill'. It can be introduced in any one of the houses where it is read thrice and debated upon; thereupon the recommended changes are included. If majority of the members of this house supports the motion in favour of the bill for all the three times, then the bill is sent to the other house. The same process is repeated here as well and if majority of the members again supports the bill all the three times, it is sent to the king or the queen. The bill becomes law only after the queen signs it. Any member belonging to either of the house can introduce a new bill but it is usually the ministers who start such motions. If any major bill brought in by any of the ministers is not sanctioned through the above mentioned process, that is, if majority of the members oppose it, then the minister resigns from the post. In such cases the houses of the parliament dissolve and new members of the House of Commons are elected by the people of the cities, districts, etc. New set of ministers are then elected from amongst these members of the parliament.

The British are divided into two main political wings. One faction is known as the 'liberals', that is progressive, and the other is called 'conservatives', that is orthodox. The Liberals want to bring in a number of progressive reforms in the government and look forward to an overall development, free from all orthodoxies. They publicly declare peace, economic restrain and development to be their primary aims.

They love to live in harmony with other races and take into account their merits and demerits as they would do in their own case. They share happiness or sorrow of people belonging to different races. But the conservatives want to preserve the present system of government the way it is. They are quite reluctant to bring in any development or change and are only concerned about the prosperity and well-being of their own country over that of the others.

Apart from these two parties, there are a few smaller ones. But most of the people either adhere to the liberals or to the conservatives. Majority of the members of the parliament belong to either of the two parties. Once a parliament is dissolved, the members of the House of Commons have to be re-elected. In that general election, if the number of liberals exceeds that of the conservatives, then the new set of ministers would be chosen from among the liberals. In such a parliament, the conservatives belonging to both the houses are called the opposition. During this period they are supposed to counter most of the bills presented by the ministers. Similarly, if after a general election, the number of members from the conservative party exceeds that of the liberals, then ministers are selected from the former group. And then in that parliament, the liberals constitute the opposition. Generally, new parliament is formed after every six or seven years and in this period the members of the House of Commons are freshly elected. If the parliament has to be dissolved before its time due to the resignation of its ministers for the reasons already mentioned above, the general election for the members of the House of Commons occur within a much shorter period of time. At least every seven years a general election has to be held because according to the government policies of this country, no parliament can function for more than seven consecutive years. It is almost impossible to describe the euphoria that accompanies any general election of this country. Indians in particular will not be able to understand it unless they are personally present here during that period.

A famous British author gave the following description of a general election of a particular city. In this city there had been a terrible commotion regarding parliamentary elections. John was the representative of the Conservatives and Smith had agreed to the request of his friends to become the representative of the Liberals. Both the candidates had issued a pamphlet each a few days back wherein they had explained about the political issues which they would support in the parliament, the parties to which they would adhere to, the ways in which they would argue for the benefit of the people of that city and other such issues. This had led to a severe factionalism in the city. Almost everyone had joined one party or the other. The liberals wore blue ribbons or carried some blue mark so they were known as the blue party and the conservatives carried some kind of red mark about their person, and were hence known as the red party.

Both the parties were trying their best to save their side. Whenever the two parties of blue and red met, whether in society or in the market-place, they had fierce rows. For every issue, whatever the blues said, the reds opposed them.

Both the parties organised meetings to praise their own and vilify the opponent. Among the four newspapers published from the city, two favoured the liberals and the other two opposed them in their bid to support the conservatives. All around the city the blue and the red flags were fluttering and on big posters written in blue or red ink, there were calls to the people of the city to support either John or Smith. Wherever you turned to see—on the windows of the shops, rooftops of houses, public vehicles or on the back of some men, everywhere there were pamphlets written in red or blue ink. The candidates were visiting all parts of the city and going for door to door campaigning to convince the people to support their candidature.

This continued for almost a month. The furore kept on mounting. Finally it was the day of the election. From the early morning itself there was a huge racket in the city. Everyone seemed to have lost their mind in their heartiest effort to make either John or Smith win the election. From early morning onwards there were sounds of drums and bugle. Roads echoed with people's shouts and sounds of vehicles. At times there were even skirmishes between two rival factions. Eventually, it was past noon. Jack and Smith talked to the people of the town for one last time. Both of them said that those who were going to support them were the wisest, most free minded, spirited, and understanding while those supporting their opponent was utterly foolish and out of their minds. They also said that they would try their best to help the city and its people, improve the trade and commerce in the city and work towards the well-being of its people. Both the parties took out large processions along with horses and carriages throughout the city. There was a large crowd on either side of the road—some cheering them up and others hooting them.

Finally it was the time for polling. The voters went to their designated places and started casting their votes for either John or Smith. Commotion plagued the town. There were huge crowd of people travelling in vehicles or there were other groups on foot, going to the site of election. Crowd jostled on roads and almost everyone was in frenzy. No one could keep silent for a moment. All around only red and blue colours were visible. The liquor shops were the most decorated ones. They had the brightest of flags fluttering over them. There was a large crowd around the building where the polling was taking place. People entered it with a lot of difficulty. The crowd kept on increasing as did disorder. People's cries became sharper.

After some time the polling was over. Suddenly everything went silent. Everybody awaited the result with abated breath. Soon the counting was over. The city's magistrate announced the result that Smith has won by a hundred votes so he would become the Member of Parliament from this area. Once again there started a terrible commotion—Smith's supporters cheered loudly for him while his opponents gave vent to their dissatisfaction in disgruntled voices. At places there were even squabbles between the two parties. Gradually confusion subsided and the crowd dispersed, each going back to their jobs. In this way the election was completed.

DAILY LIFE

In England there is a vast difference in the daily lives of the rich, the middle class and the poor. Most of the gentlemen get up by half past eight in the morning and take their 'breakfast' around nine o'clock. This is not an elaborate fare. They have butter toast, boiled egg, fish, sometimes a little meat, and tea or coffee. After breakfast, the master of the house leaves for work. The mistress of the house then either looks after the household or occupies herself with her dresses. At one o'clock they take their lunch which is a light repast. The English people living in India call this meal 'tiffin'. During lunch they take bread and butter along with some meat and a couple of glasses of liquor. Most of the men take their lunch at their workplaces. Post lunch, the women go out, either to their friends' place or for shopping etc. Dinner is the chief meal of this country. The rich ones take their dinner between six or seven o'clock in the evening. The cook spends at least four to five hours to prepare various delicacies and the maid or a servant lays the table. The table is covered with a table cloth on which cutlery, glasses, etc are neatly arranged. Food is brought in only when it is dinner time and a bell is rung to inform the family members that the dinner is ready to be served. Then one by one the master of the household, the mistress and their children take their seats; but before they do so the master says the 'grace' which is an offering to the God. It is only after that the dinner begins. There is no stipulated duration for this meal. In some of the families, people finish eating within an hour and there are some others who keep on gorging on meat and liquor through a couple of hours. Dinner is an elaborate affair. There is a variety of food—soup, fish, roasted or fried meat, potatoes, vegetables, sweets, fruits and liquor. Prior to dinner, all the members of the family wash themselves and wear nice clothes. In most of the upper class houses, dressing up for the dinner is a grand affair. The rich ladies often take up about two to three hours to get ready for the dinner. This might amuse us but great people have their own fancies; and particularly so, when dressing up is one of the chief preoccupations of the women here.

After dinner the entire family gathers in the drawing room and engages in conversation, plays music or reads books and newspapers. When I see parents along with their grown up or young children sitting together and enjoying themselves in simple conversations, it seems to me that the everyday lives of the unfortunate Indians are truly devoid of all such pleasures. In India we do not have this system of taking our meals together or spending some time with the entire family. Here, the head of the family has a separate meal, his wife hides herself in some part of the house and satiates her hunger, the grown up boys rush through their own meals at some another time. Women of the household remain satisfied with whatever is given to them as charity and the smaller children come under no special treatment. In our country, we do not have any tradition of the family members sitting together for a chat. At nine o'clock in the evening the rich Englishmen have tea with an occasional biscuit or two. After that they again go back to their own work. After two more hours, around eleven, most of the Englishmen go to bed.

The middle class and the poor here wake up at six or seven in the morning and take a sparse meal of bread, butter, egg, etc. Thereafter, the men go out to work and the women get busy with their household chores. They have to do a lot of work by themselves and many cannot afford to keep a single maid. The middleclass people take their dinner by one or two in the afternoon. The poor take it even earlier. Though dinner is the chief meal of the day, it is not an elaborate affair for them. They generally have roasted meat, boiled potatoes, some sweets and beer. Most of the workers come home for dinner and thereafter go back to their jobs. Women, after finishing the rest of their domestic chores, get dressed up and either do some needlework or go out for some work. When the men return from their work at around six or seven in the evening, all the members of the family gather to have their tea along with some bread and butter, etc. After that they chat among themselves or read newspapers and relax. They take their 'supper' at around nine or ten at night. This class has simple fares for their supper, such as meat, potatoes or bread. They go off to sleep around ten o' clock.

This is how the British people spend their daily lives. Under no circumstances would they deviate from this routine, not even in case of an accident in the family. Such a disciplined life not only keeps them healthy, it also saves a lot of time and does not allow any indiscipline in the family. Since we do not maintain any such discipline in our everyday affairs we keep on getting into some scrapes or the other. We always hear about complaints and grudges pertaining to disorderliness of the Bengali family—some day someone has to go to office hungry because the rice is not cooked at proper time; or the head of the family gets very angry because the evening meal is not prepared at the correct time. Indian women have no fixed time for their meals. If one day they take their food at around ten in the morning, the next day it can be late afternoon. But as the British have a fixed time for their meals, one does not come across such problems in their families.

When someone comes here from India for the first time, he is surprised to see the bolted doors of all the houses irrespective of their social status. It would appear that people have locked their houses and have gone visiting some other country. But that is not the case. It is the custom of this country to keep the main entrance shut. They do so either because of the cold climate or for their safety in such lonely surroundings. The front door is fitted with an iron hammer called a 'knocker'. A number of houses have both a knocker and a bell. If someone wants to enter a house or call anyone, he will have to either beat the door with a knocker or ring the bell. In order to avoid confusion they have assigned different styles of knocking for different types of people. If any gentleman or a friend comes, he knocks the door three to four times. The postman raps twice rapidly, and the hawkers, servants or maids rap only once. The people within can guess the kind of person knocking their door. So they can get prepared accordingly and open the door at the earliest.

A middle class British house consists of a drawing room, dining room, and according to the size of the family five or six bedrooms, a kitchen and a room for washing clothes. There is also a small courtyard just in front of the main door, a cellar and a room for utensils in the front and a small garden at the back of the house. The size of the room and its purpose is decided during the construction of the house itself. And the rooms are constructed accordingly. Therefore there is neither any unutilised space within the house, nor any confusion regarding the use of the rooms. In addition, the rich people have a big drawing room, reading room, a room for smoking, a chamber for clothes, wine cellar and servants' rooms in addition to those mentioned earlier. Some houses also have a glass-room, known as 'conservatory' to grow flowering plants at home. Nowadays, a number of houses also have a bathroom. The British generally do not have the provision for taking bath.

Some among the affluent class have started taking bath, a practice that they have learnt from other races. Probably due to cold or just because of their whim, the lower class people of England are extremely dirty. I doubt whether they clean themselves even once a month. Apart from the rich Englishmen, the middleclass or lower class people do not have any provision for bath. Nowadays there are a few common baths in London and other big cities meant for the common people. Everyone can go there and bathe as much as they want to. But these baths are quite expensive. To take a bath in one of the first class facilities, one might have to pay between six annas to one rupee, depending on its type, and from two to six annas for the second grade ones.

Houses in England are not as big as those in our country. Since a number of houses stand together, they appear huge. But generally, they are not more than thirty feet wide. Their exteriors are not much impressive as well. Walls are not whitewashed, and they do not even have blinds or a window. Except the larger ones, most houses here are made of bricks and wood, fitted with glass windows.

The interior looks quite nice. Most of the houses have a staircase running right from the bottom to its topmost floor. They are usually made of wood, except in a few big houses where they are built with stones. Their floors are of wooden planks and there are wall papers on all the walls. All the rooms have a fireplace where they light a fire during winter. Just above the fireplace is a mantelpiece. In posh houses they are made of marble. In our country one can at least count the joist or rafters in the ceiling when one is idle. But here even that is not possible because the ceilings are either plain or at times have some floral design in the centre. While constructing, they first place the joists and then instead of rafters and tiles they fix wooden planks on both the sides. Then they make the ceiling strong with lime and sand filling. In the entire house, only the roofs are whitewashed. The doors do not have double panes as we have in our country; instead they have a single large door. There is not any threshold too and in place of a chain and a latch, the doors have a bronze handle and a lock fitted to its surface. Only the main entrance and the door to the garden have iron bolts or big latches. The roof is set on a number of small joists. They do not have tiles or stone chips as we have in Bengal. The houses in England look quite strong from the outside but after staying in them for a while we can understand how weak they are. If a strong wind blows as it does in India, all these houses will topple down within an hour or two. Generally the houses have thin walls and a shallow foundation. The joists are thin as well and instead of bricks, stone chips and lime mixture; they only exhaust loads of wood.

Unlike in India, they do not have to shout themselves hoarse to call their servants. There is a brass handle fitted in the wall near the fireplace in every room. These handles are connected to a number of bells in the ground floor. Each room is connected to a separate bell. So the moment anyone pushes the handle, the maids and servants can identify the room and immediately rush into that room. But the British are not satisfied even with this. With newer developments in Science, they try to make their lives as comfortable as possible. Nowadays, some of the houses have an electronic switch instead of such bells. If a person presses a button on a wall of the house, a bell rings downstairs.

The decor of the houses displays their love for comfort and their increasing foppery. Everywhere the prosperous is inclined towards luxury, but here, in England, even the most average household has a carpet, a sofa set, a mahogany table, a piano, a nice cupboard, full-size mirrors, pictures, chandeliers and many such expensive and lavish items. In addition to these, the houses are stuffed with various other furnishings. If you visit the house of even a humble carpenter or a blacksmith, you will find a carpet on the floor of the drawing room, a nice window curtain and a table cover, a sofa set, a shelf, a picture, clock and other such things. The room will be neat and clean. When it comes to the decoration of the house, the poor people try and imitate their social superiors. The latter in turn look up to those even more affluent than they are. Thus, even the poor here learn profligacy. What is considered a luxury in our country, here is taken to be a necessity even among the poor. Some of the houses of the common middleclass people appear more luxurious than the houses of the rich people of our country. The worth of decorating a ten-roomed house in the British style is about a thousand rupees.

I shall attempt a brief description of the British kitchen to substantiate their love for a comfortable living. I have already stated that most of the kitchens are in the basement and do not get much light or air. But their kitchens are much tidier than even our bedrooms. They do not use mud or brick *unoon* as used by us for cooking. Attached to a wall is an iron stove which is lighted with the help of paper, small pieces of wood or coal. There is a chimney enclosed within that wall with an opening at the roof which is used to vent out the smoke. Whether rich or poor, every household has proper facilities. Kitchens vary according to the lifestyle though at times they go beyond their means. Everyone except the lowest class of people keep their kitchen clean. All the necessary things needed in a kitchen are kept within or near it. They do not have to run around to find the required items. In most of the houses kitchen floor is covered with old rugs and are furnished with a table, a cot, etc. They also have racks along the walls for crockery and other utensils. In one of the corners there is a tap and a small tank underneath it. The kitchen walls have neither cobwebs nor oil stains and the floor is clean. Things are neatly arranged and kept in their proper places. In some of the houses, there are couches, cupboards, pictures and books as well in the kitchen. Here the poor and the middle class people take their meals in the kitchen itself. Though the British lack in personal hygiene[xlvii], they are extremely disciplined and tidy in all other aspects is worth praising.

Compared to India, almost everything is more expensive here. Firstly, England is a very small island; to add to that, most of the available land is either used up by mining industries, or have become hunting grounds for the rich people, or are utilised as pastures for the cattle. A lot of care and hard work is required to make the land fertile and yielding. So it is quite natural that things will be more expensive here. I have heard that about fifty years ago, things such as bread were three to four times costlier than today. They had to pay a very heavy duty for things imported from other countries. So, even if the foreign goods came for a cheap price, due to such duty, it was not at all profitable to sell them in England. Gradually, the British abolished this import duty. Since then, with the presence of imported items, indigenous productions from the newly set up industries and a competitive market, thing have become much cheaper. In the process food has become affordable. Even then if we compare the prices of commodities between England and our country, everything appears much costlier here. These days, food items have become widely available as they have started importing a number of things like wheat, potato, eggs etc. If we look at the British population and the sparse amount of food products produced here, it becomes evident that England will not be able to sustain itself even for six months if its relationship with all other countries gets disrupted. It will surely face a famine.

Among food crops, they grow wheat, barley, and oat in huge quantities. They grow some peas and beans as well. But apart from these, things such as rice, pulses, sago, etc, which are crops of warmer countries, are imported either from America or Asia. Here the best quality rice costs about seven annas per ser and the inferior varieties are around three annas. The price, though shocking to us is not at all high if we consider the whole situation. They have to bring these from far off lands like India or America, and then they have to store them properly in a clean place. The rice here is so clean that once bought it can be cooked even without a wash. This saves a lot of effort and time. Many vegetable grow here and some are imported from foreign lands as well. Vegetables such as potatoes, onions or cabbages are available throughout the year. Those vegetables that grow in our country in the winters, such as green peas, radish, cauliflower, french beans, etc are available here in the summers. Potatoes of good quality cost about six or seven paise a kilogram and one cabbage comes for around five paise. At times vegetables are even cheaper. The fruits available here are no match for those found in our country, but here one can find a few varieties of small delicious fruits throughout the year. Their chief fruits are strawberry, guava, grapes, apple, pomegranate, etc. A huge quantity of oranges is imported from Spain. Fruits are more expensive here but there is nothing that is not available. Certain varieties of Indian fruits, such as pineapple, banana, coconut, etc are also found here. These are imported from America. They are exorbitantly priced and do not even taste good.

Shopping is an enjoyable activity here in spite of the fact that most commodities are quite expensive. One can enjoy shopping here in spite of the fact that most of the things are more expensive in this country. The British values both money and time. Unlike in our country, here there is no scope for bargaining. In India, even to buy something trivial, we have to haggle a lot over its price. An hour long bargaining might help us to buy an item priced at one rupee for say, six annas. Yet, the suspicion of being cheated lurks in our minds. In the process we waste a lot of time and gain a headache. Here such situations never occur. Customers are not plagued by fear of dishonest shopkeepers and do not have to argue with them for every small thing they buy. There are various kinds of shops on either side of the road, very close to the houses. When you need something, you go to a shop; the shopkeeper offers you two or three options. You only have to select the one you need and pay its actual price. The whole transaction gets over in five minutes. There is no argument or any other hassle. The shops are so clean and beautifully decorated that even the richest of the society will not hesitate to visit it. In our country, a look at the grocer's shop is enough to put such people off. As it is, all the items are kept in the open and are quite untidy. To add to it, oil leaks from jars, salt becomes damp, flies hover over jugs of molasses. A mere look will keep the gentlemen away from these shops. Here, be it the grocer, green grocer or the fish monger, each keeps the shop spic and span. No woman, irrespective of her social or economic status, feels it beneath her dignity to do her own shopping. Once you buy anything, the shopkeeper delivers it to your home. So ladies don't have to bother regarding carrying goods by themselves. The food needed for daily consumption, such as bread, milk, potato, vegetables, meat, are delivered at doorstep by the shopkeepers going around in hand pulled rickshaw or horse drawn carriage.

Generally, the food items here are of superior quality and taste good, though they are priced quite high. The breads which are a bit bigger in size cost ten paisa, but such fresh and delicious bread is not available even in the best of British hotels in our country. The butter that we get here is also of a good quality. Moreover since this is a cold country, butter remains fresh for a longer time. It is not the milk white variety that we get in Bengal; but yellowish in colour. It costs between one rupee and twelve annas to two rupees and four annas. In Bombay a similar variety of butter is available but I have never seen such in Calcutta. Perhaps, the milk is creamier here, so the butter that is made from it is of such a superior quality. Milk generally costs about fourteen paise per ser[xlviii]. Unlike India, here ghee is not available. They mostly use lard for cooking purposes; at times they also use oil or butter. Here there are various kinds of sugar. The variety that is generally used is similar to the one that we see in our country—white and clean, but it has smaller granules. It costs about six annas per ser. For cooking, they use a kind of brownish powdered sugar which is imported from the United States of America and costs about five annas per ser. The molasses that is available here is of a very poor quality. Honey is delicious but very expensive. Various spices like turmeric, chilli, coriander, small cardamoms, etc are imported from India. But they are highly expensive; about sixty grams cost four annas. Salt is very cheap here—three paise per ser. Unlike in India, here the British do not impose heavy taxes to rob the poor even of their salt.

Compared to India, fish here is neither good in taste nor rich in variety. In summer salmons are available; these are quite big and taste good. They resemble the *rohu* fish of our country and cost about one and a half rupee per ser. There are a few varieties of smaller fish as well but we found them quite tasteless and expensive. Whether due to its high price or some other reasons, people here are not much fond of fish. Big built British crave only for meat. I have seen huge crabs and lobsters here. A huge crab resembles a tortoise. The British prefer beef, veal and pork more. Veal is very soft and delicious. One can even fry it in four to five minutes and have it. Beef is the national food for the British. I have heard that England has the best quality beef. The poor people mostly consume pork because it is the cheapest available meat. Different types of domestic animals like chicken, duck and rabbit are also available but they are found only on the rich men's platter. The chicken which costs about four annas in our country would cost no less than two rupees here.

I hope by now my readers have realised that surviving here is a costly affair. In most of the countries, food items are cheaper in villages than in cities. But as the British import most of these items, they are more easily available in the cities. Therefore, in this country, though land and property are cheaper in the country side, the cost of living is not less than that of the cities. In this country of extreme cold and frequently changing climactic condition, one has to spend a lot on clothes. In England, a rough estimate shows that a poor person spends between fifteen to forty rupees a month on housing, food and clothes. Those who belong to the lower economic group spend around fifty to hundred per month while the middle class has to spend between hundred and hundred and fifty rupees. Over and above this amount, whatever one spends becomes a marker of that person's wealth. The cost of living reduces if four to five persons stay together like a family. But this estimation does not include educational and other expenses.

THE HARD WORKING BRITISH—CRAFTSMEN—TRADE—WORKERS

The British are famous throughout the world for their hard work and this is the best quality that a race can possess. If you read their history, you will see that all their achievements are testimonies of their hard work. Today their hard work exists as a model everywhere. It is due to this industrious nature that in such a short time they have transformed themselves from a barbaric tribe who lived in forests to one of the most cultured races of the world. And it is the hard work of the common people that has sowed the seeds of British greatness. In short, the British have achieved everything including their wealth, freedom and empire by dint of this particular quality. Prosperity of the entire nation has been achieved through every individual's uncompromising commitment towards their tasks however difficult they might be. The main cause of this prosperity is the physical and mental labour of various people—such as that of farmers, manufacturers of essential goods, inventors and makers of weapons and machines, authors, artisans, etc. Diligence is not only the lifeline of the British race; it is also the chief means by which they rectify their faults. If they find themselves lagging behind any of the races in any affair, they try their best to improve themselves in that field. Also, if they can locate any fault within their administrative system, they are never too lazy to ignore it; instead, they try their best to set it right.

The industrious nature of most of the British amazes us. Here, I have often read about such men who in spite of their birth in poor and lowly families have rose to fame and prosperity by their sheer hard work. Invention of steam engine has helped a number of races around the world. It has also made British industrial production and trade and commerce easier and faster. It was the working class people who invented this useful steam engine. Famous inventors like Newcomen, Smeaton, James Watt, and others were coppersmiths, carpenters or mere labourers in their early life. Among the contemporary renowned people of this country, there are many who had ascended to their social position through sheer hard work. Some British authors work hard for about twenty to twenty five years at a stretch in order to write a book well and become successful. Some spend their entire life and money for the sake of their inventions. Generally, the British are found to be more focused and hard working when it comes to industry and trade than most other races. The British are never idle, either due to climate or out of their natural disposition.

Industriousness has been the best means of British education. Their commendable progress from an ignorant race to a knowledgeable one has been only due to toil and labour. Some poets say that slog and suffering are the only means of attaining heaven. Truly, there is nothing sweeter than the fruits of one's own labour. Human civilization could have been possible because of this reason. Many people consider laziness to be the actual bliss and hard work to be the bane of life. But if they think carefully, they will realise that just as the body becomes inactive if all its parts are not in action, human beings become dull in absence of any activity.

The ability to work is a gift of God and it is this gift which has enabled the British to undertake all difficult and arduous tasks. It is because of this gift that they have remained engaged in trade and industrialization and thus surpassed many other races. The British had first come to India for trading purposes. It is trade that has led England to unfurl its flag in all parts of the world. On the other hand, see how weak we Indians have become in absence of any hard work. Our indolence has cost us all our wealth, respect, etc. and it is our contempt for physical labour that has left us far behind other civilized races. In spite of watching the way foreigners are appropriating our trade and industry entirely and how they are draining away our blood, we are not conscious. This is how supine we have become!!^{xlix}

It is amazing to note how the British have made gradual progress in industrialisation. At one point of time when France, Spain, Holland, Belgium and some other European countries were setting up industries to make silk gloves, socks etc, England did not have any source of livelihood except agriculture. Such a situation continued even long after. In those days the British used to exchange their indigenous products to get silk from the foreigners. They remained contented to either buy silk garments or buy silk thread and then weave them into clothes in small quantities. Later, with the rise of Protestantism, many hard working Western Europeans who had gone through religious conversion, had to escape from their homelands. When they found a refuge in England, they were glad to set up those industries here and teach the British this new craft in return for their hospitality. This was the beginning of industrialisation in England. Eventually steam engine was invented. This invention coupled with British hard work and skill has made England unparalleled in industrialisation.

Cotton is their prime industry. They import raw cotton from countries like America and India, stitch them into garments which they later export to various countries. By the end of the year 1874, England and Ireland together had about two thousand and seven hundred cotton factories. Among its employees, one lakh eighty-eight thousand were men and the rest were women. Manchester is the hub of these industries. After cotton, fur and woollen garments manufacturing industries came next in importance. Till the end of the above mentioned year, there were eighteen hundred fur industries and about seven hundred wool industries and about two lakhs and eighty thousand people worked in all these. England imports most of its cotton from other countries but wool is primarily available here. Leeds, a city in the northern part of England is the chief place for wool industries. England also makes various other kinds of garments and other necessary textile materials such as silk materials, jute items, socks, lace, etc.

The owners of these factories in England are almost like emperors. Like monarchs they have immense wealth, various ambitions, huge enterprises, threat and apprehension as well as pride and conceit. They too send their ambassadors and representatives to different parts of the world; keep a track of the condition and needs of the people living in the nearby or far-off countries; they rule over the working class and take into account their conditions. If they so wish, they can help a large number of people. In short, they are the masters controlling human labour. They generally deal in crores in their business. The stockpiles in their godowns appear well beyond belief. There is no place in the world, such as, India, China, Japan, Australia, Egypt, and South America, where you will not find their representatives. They gather information about the various items that are used and are in demand in those countries and send it to England. Those things are manufactured in the factories here and exported to the respective countries. In India we always come across new products manufactured in England. It seems that the Indians have stopped using their handloom products. This is because the clever British gets hold of samples of all kinds of clothes used in our country and then manufacture exactly similar ones here and send them back to India. Though these machine-made clothes have not been able to surpass the quality of our handloom products such as sari, shawls and other items, they are manufactured at such a low cost that the poor Indians have gradually started preferring them.

British trade and commerce truly leaves us astonished. The godowns have fur garments stored in heaps as high as hills. There is a godown at Leeds which has a space of about 200 yards in the front and it is so high that a steam engine has to be used to stack or bring down a bundle of wool from its place at the top of the heap. In a cotton factory at

Manchester, about three lakhs shuttles are used. It has been recorded that the only cotton yarn and clothes produced in Manchester earns a profit of twelve crores. A single 'company' earns a profit of about two lakh rupees a month and employs about five thousand people. All these companies have a huge capital. They use machines of superior quality and have excellent arrangements. The employees are skilled and hard working. All the labourers, supervisors and clerks work with discipline and dedication.

I have already discussed the impact of iron and hard coal upon this country. Without these mineral resources, England could not have achieved even one percent of prosperity that it enjoys today. All the industries are completely dependent on iron and coal. There are in all about fourteen coal mines here, of these the ones in the north are larger. A single field spreads up to twenty to twenty four miles. These fields are full of deep mines. There are four hundred and thirty pits for digging out coal and innumerable number of people working in these. Apart from iron, England also has substantial amount of other minerals such as tin, copper, etc. Just as Manchester has a number of cotton mills, Birmingham is full of huge iron and brass factories which produce excellent iron implements. Necessary items such as iron nails or hinges made in England are found all over the world. There are many millionaires involved in this trade and each of them is perhaps richer than the kings in our country. One of the masons here has become very affluent through his business in screws and has eventually become very influential. Many of you must have seen the name Sheffield on British knives and scissors. That place is famous for manufacturing all kinds of sharp tools. Apart from the things that I have just mentioned above, England also manufactures various other items; machines, ships, furniture, crockery to name a few. I shall have to write three to four voluminous books for a detailed discussion on each of these.

Like industries, trade is another important source of income here. In this they are second to none. There are no such ports where one does not see a British ship. Standing near dock, which is the hub of ships in London it seems that all the wealth of the world sails into England and gets accumulated at her feet. London has six such docks. All of them are vast and at the very first sight look like huge treasure-houses. Each of the docks resembles a big port and is almost always crowded with a number of ships. Stand aside and look at the boats sailing in all directions and ships waiting in queues. It seems that they have raised their heads above water to proclaim to the world the extent of British industriousness and mercantile power. One has come from Russia carrying freight of about eighty maundsl, a certain other has come from India, another from Africa or America, carrying various kinds of merchandise within them. None contain less than ninety to hundred maunds. Anyone looking at all these mercantile ships, assembling from all the four quarters of the world, will be amazed at the British industriousness. According to the records in a year about forty thousand ships visit these docks and at a time there are about five to six thousand of them plying on the river Thames or docked in London. It sends shivers down the spines to even think of the amount of wealth these ships extort from other countries.

London and Liverpool are the places for international trade. They mainly import items such as food grains, flour, cotton, wool, sugar, tea, coffee, wood, etc. The items which they export to other countries are chiefly cotton and woollen textiles, thread, iron and steel products, coal, weapons of various kinds, machines and tools, etc. There are twenty thousand sail ships assigned for this purpose and about one lakh and forty thousand people employed in these. There are about three thousand steam ships and about sixty eight thousand people work there. Apart from these British also have a number of war-ships which employ a huge number of people.

After reading all these perhaps my readers have understood why there are so many rich people in England and the factors responsible for their immense wealth. The amount of wealth earned by one British merchant is often more than the accumulated wealth of a number rich Indians. British money has been invested to set up industries in many other countries. In India, the capital investment for all the railway companies has come from England. They have also invested their money in other countries such as Russia, Turkey, Africa, Canada, Brazil, etc. There are about two hundred banks in London and at least two to three each in all other cities have.

These banks are store-houses of money. Here money comes from all over the world and from here again they are sent to various countries in huge quantities. Here everyone—

landlord, trader, shopkeeper, doctor, barrister or government employee, keep money in banks. Again it is this money which helps in the running of all kinds of trade and commerce, industries, companies, etc. In this country money is never left idle. England is the best example of money begetting money.

If you stroll along the roads of the important cities in England you will realise that there are number of rich people living here. A journey of four to six miles by a car in certain areas of London brings to our view huge buildings on both sides of the road. The houses proudly holding their heads high stand as a proof of their owners' wealth. None of these people earn less than two to three thousand rupees a month. All the houses have stable, horses, carriages, grooms, coachman and other servants. All these houses are furnished with expensive furniture and other precious items in these houses. Here, the doctors, barristers and other professionals earn more than their counterparts in other countries. In our country one can pay two to four rupees to a general physician for a home visit but one has to pay a fee of not less than twelve rupees for the same in England. The distinguished professors at Oxford and Cambridge earn about two to three thousand rupees a month. I have heard that though the poet laureate Tennyson receives a small salary from the royal treasury, he earns even up to five thousand a month for the poems that he writes. The proprietor of The Times, the most popular British daily, pays even a thousand rupees for the articles of excellence that are published in it. The clerk who earns a monthly salary of thirty rupees in India has his equivalent here earning about a hundred and fifty rupees a month. But just as the people earn more here, they also have a lot of expenses. After looking at everything it seems that spending commensurate one's income here. After reading this section on British wealth I hope my readers are not persuaded into thinking that everything is bright and beautiful here, you must remember that there are always two sides of a coin.

There are many big and small factories, workshops and similar units of production that provide for a huge number of people. I have told earlier that they have a wonderful system here. The labourers are very hard working and trust worthy. They can very cleverly replicate from a model. In an iron factory a skilled worker can earn up to eighty or ninety rupees a month. Even the ones who are not so skilled earn about forty rupees a month. Women and children earn about twenty-five rupees per month. In the cotton factories at Lancashire, a young labourer has a monthly salary of fifty rupees. In this country all the workers earn as much as or even more than the clerks in India. Even the sweepers and other such workers get no less than fifteen or sixteen rupees per month.

In spite of earning more, the poor people of this country are not well-off in terms of money or their lifestyle. The reason behind this is extravagance. They are spendthrifts and in addition to it, here most of the things are quite expensive. So they have a high domestic expense. One who earns about eight rupees a month can spend a sort of comfortable life in our country, but here even after earning twenty five rupees per month one has to lead a miserable life. One has to spend a lot on coal, light, alcohol and meat. Even the poor people here cannot survive just on vegetables, without meat and alcohol, so it is not surprising that they cannot sustain themselves with the money they earn. Also, though they do not have the custom of child marriage, the working class people have many children. Almost every family has four to five children. In this cold country with its fluctuating weather, the poor labourer has to struggle hard just to provide food and clothes for the family.

Now many measures are being taken to improve the conditions of these working class people here. They are given lessons in politics and are keen learners. In many places these uneducated or little educated and physically exhausted people gather together to form societies where they discuss and debate upon political and other issues and are quite knowledgeable about the affairs of other places. Some libraries with public funding have been established for these people where they can read various kinds of books and newspapers for free. There are a number of places where they can receive education for nominal fees. The workers, after returning from their work in the evening, go to these places to learn various subjects. Here men and women are at par in learning to sing, play instruments, paint, knit and stitch garments.

LAST WORDS

I have seen many new things here, learnt about new subjects, and gained new knowledge; but the more I see and learn, more the time I spend here, greater is my sorrow for India. The more I compare the two countries, starker I find the contrast between the two. Now I can better understand the wretched condition of India and it gives me a lot of pain. At times I lose all hopes of India's ever being able to regain her happiness and at times I can see some rays of hope. I think some of my fellow countrymen are also going through the same feelings as mine; many of them are suffering like me for the degenerated condition of the country. Such people can come forward to work for the betterment of the country once they clearly understand the merits and demerits of the two countries.

By reading the sections on British education, trade and women's education, every Indian will realise how much superior England is to India. Similarly, on reading about the British society, domestic life, the individual's love for independence, patriotism, self-respect, etc., they can see how much the British life is different from that of ours. We are the children of the ancient Hindus of the Aryavartya—those who in the ancient past, even before the Greeks, had been famous throughout the world for their civilization, spirituality and education; those who were unparalleled in their devotion to dharma, truth and their control over five senses. In fact, when all the civilized countries of the world were practicing slavery, then only the Hindus had condemned this hateful practice and abstained from keeping a man enslaved for life. The fame of their brave deeds had spread throughout the world. Various civilized races of the world have learnt ancient Mathematics, Astronomy and Philosophy from us and are now becoming famous by their new inventions and discoveries. We are the descendents from that race of Hindus, then why are we in such a state today? Why are we wandering in wretched condition in our own country, deprived of our spirit, strength, wealth, fame, freedom and all happiness? Today, why do we consider Calcutta more significant than Kashi, Prayag, Mathura and other such places which were pillars of Hinduism? Everybody knows the answer yet no one is willing to say so or even listen about it. But no one can deny the fact that we ourselves are responsible for this current state. In no way are the British physically different or better than us. Is not this current state of subservience a fault of our own?

We are the daughters of those Hindu women who had encouraged their husbands to go to the battlefield and did not hesitate a bit to sacrifice their own lives on the pyre to preserve their honour and chastity. Their brave deeds echoed throughout the world and they became symbols of dharma, satitva and courageousness. Yet today our place is at the feet of our subjugators; is it not our fault—the children of India? Today, where is the Indian woman's courage and pride in her Dharma? Once we used to proclaim "let us sell all our meaningless jewellery to buy provision for our soldiers" but where is that pledge now? In spite of seeing our men sitting idle like cowards, do we have the power any longer to enthuse them into some action? There is nothing left for us. We have lost everything due to our own faults. Lack of unity like a poisonous viper has brought our doom. It is this lack of unity that has divided our country into various fragments and made us subjects first under the Muslims and then under the British. On the other hand it is this unity that has made it possible for the British, inhabitants of a very small island, to easily defeat a much bigger country like Hindustan and rule over it successfully. Due to our sectarianism we have become pauper and completely spineless. In spite of being a civilised race we are considered uncivilised as we are under foreign rule. Termites, though minute in size, build a large mound collectively and when disturbed by human beings, they put up a united front to confront them. They are not afraid even though the human beings are much bigger than them. Yet, we who are facing oppressors whose physical appearances are same as ours, are scared to resist them because of lack of unity.

There was a time when the Hindus were revered throughout the world as the very resource of civilization and knowledge. But now the people belonging to the independent nations dismiss the subjugated Indians as uncivilized, spiritless and cowardly. Though we are creatures of flesh and blood, we easily bear with these insults and do not react. Are not these our faults? Bengalis in particular, are the most knowledgeable and intelligent among all other Indian races but they are extremely coward and timid. Then what is the need for such knowledge? None of the people of the other regions of India are as subservient as the Bengalis when they encounter a British, neither do they prostrate themselves at the feet of a foreign race.

These are the very men who are oppressive towards their women. The educated Bengali youth is busy earning degrees and in pursuit of their own pleasure; silent tears of the caged Bengali women fail to draw their attention. British women are trying their best for their right to vote to elect the members of parliament; if we could similarly fight for women's liberation here and drive it straight into the hearts of every Indian or instead of repressing our desires, we could shout our hearts out in front of our men, then perhaps we could make our Bengali brothers lend an ear to our sufferings. But we have lost all the spirit and strength for an independent life due to years of servitude. That is why now we are not able to fight with all our might like the British women to be equal to the men of our society.

This country has many enjoyable sights but the ones that I prefer most are the mixed gatherings of men and women, their playing together, adult women marching to school, etc. Which Indian woman will not feel contented to see men and women going for a stroll, playing, or laughing like brothers and sisters? But their happiness does not make us forget our miseries; it reinforces them. The more I see the expression of happiness on the faces of the British ladies here, the more I am reminded of the humble and tired faces of the subjugated Indian women.

Many races lack strength, intelligence or unity but with the help of a strong patriotic feeling they have succeeded in retrieving themselves from their wretched condition. But we do not even know what patriotism is. We go on with our lives normally in spite of watching the miserable condition of our country. And even after witnessing the reign of tyranny, we are not agitated enough to give up our selfish, luxurious pursuits. Like animals everyone is concerned with personal happiness only, completely oblivious of the well-being of the country. We never think deeply about things which will help the country to progress further or things that might hamper it.

In conclusion, I would like to say that in the present times it is more advisable to think of the present and the future and not go into unnecessary boasting about the past. Wise man understands history and treads cautiously in to present and future. We can get the actual picture of the present by looking at both our country and the foreign ones. Ways to improve our present and future state should be our constant thought and course of action. A historical analysis of all the civilized and prosperous races shows that there has been a constant change among them. With gradual change over a course of time they have transformed themselves a lot to become a developed country. It is also evident that those races which have remained static have gradually degenerated. Like human beings, animals and plants also constantly evolve; it is also one of the chief duties of the races to constantly modify themselves. So there is only one way to solve the present miserable state of our country—change and development.

Many people keep shouting for freedom and also unnecessarily excite others about it; but we must first contemplate whether we truly deserve to be free, whether we shall be able to maintain that state of freedom and most importantly, whether we have the strength to attain that freedom. Before attaining something it is important to find and follow the ways to attain it. We must first think out clearly whether we have the qualities of that race which we want to defeat and whether we have inculcated that strength, knowledge and means with which they have managed to rule us. If we do not have these than we must stop our tall claims and first try our best to inculcate those qualities and weed out all our superstitious and harmful traditions.

I have left all my friends and relations to live in this foreign land. It was very difficult to leave my motherland and come here. There is no such hope that I shall even get to see the land of my birth and my dear family again. Since many days my mind is agitated with various kinds of thoughts and at times it becomes difficult to contain my heart's anguish and misgivings. Since my arrival in England these sufferings have doubled and that is why I have tried to express a part of it in this book and console myself. If people of my country dislike any part of this book, I hope they would pardon me, considering that one who cries hardest is the one who feels the pain most. There are many others who could have written such a text in a much better language or expressed themselves in richer vocabulary but nobody could have experienced the intense suffering this Bengali lady, living in a foreign land, had gone through. Readers, both men and women, please

discard sections of this book which you deem unfit and accept
if there is anything worthy in it. If this book is able to
generate new perceptions or help reconsider the issues of
swadesh and *videsh*, then I shall consider all my efforts fruitful.

Oh ma! To England, a free country
I have arrived, with a hopeful heart
to find everlasting peace.
      Yet Mother India! Where can happiness be found?

Songs of freedom in the air,
and happy people all around,
shatter my heart to a hundred pieces,
      and I drown myself in my tears.

Look at England, your daughter like
so small in size yet such prowess
in strength, courage, spirit, terrifies the world
all human beings are scared
      to encounter her brave sons.

But no one is scared of us,
finding spineless, they chase us away.
Ma, they take away all your wealth
      and bind your hands in chain.

And then to see these spirited souls
their happiness, wealth and fame,
this life appears hateful

in this disgraceful bonded state.

Had you been devoid of beauty
like a vast stretch of desert,
that too was better than bondage
of what use is this life without respect
        only the weak tolerates disgrace.

Or it would have been better ma!
Had we remained in grave ignorance
like the Zulus uncivilised
but with our freedom intact
        even that would not be ignominious.

What use is so much of knowledge
being civilized, or wearing fine clothes
without possessing that priceless gem,
that which is most valuable in this world
        it will only increase heartache.

From such a distance it is
easier to see your miseries.
Oh but that only redoubles
my heart's pain.
        Oh ma, this unbearable Bengali life!

Hence I think the best would be
to stay drowned in sea of ignorance
then at least with a broken heart

I would not have to cry all day
              living so far, in free England.

Look at the immense wealth
that has sailed to English soil
from India, making her
a complete pauper forever.
                    Never shall they go back to us.

Look at their flag again
fluttering proudly on palace top
within sits the empress who
is ruling India and England.
                    wearing Kohinoor in her crown.

The Kohinoor that belonged to you
how it reached the heart of England—
this thought brings to my mind
the whole trajectory of history
                    and my heart fills with pain.

Goddess of Britain does not do
any injustice to you.
Yet to think that on her forehead
shines the Ranjit—jewel
                    makes my blood boil in anger.

And look at these sons of England
rich owners of a free heart

walks in pride, like heroes such as
the steadfast Karna, Duryodhan or Bheem
             they lead a life of bliss.

Look at the fair-skinned women here
roam around in happiness and pride.
Chain of bondage cannot bind
ever their feet, their ever smiling
             face radiant in courageous shine.

Yet, if I search the high Himalayas
or in the Vindhyas or Kanyakumari
not a single brave soul I find
is born out of your womb
             India lives on in disgrace.

On one side, cries Punjab
on the other, Maharashtra cries
while Bengal sits all alone
and cries to see her educated sons
             indifferent to their mother's suffering.

Look at our *sati-sadhwi*
who knows no more than shedding tears
distraught at her widowhood
that cast her childhood life in grief
she sobs in her lonely cottage
leaving all happiness and hope
             yet that bond she cannot untie.

Elsewhere a daughter of India
deep in sorrow, quietly thinks
in bondage everyone lives
yet it drives her mad to think
whoever thinks of their suffering
or even take a look at them,
            wrapped always in superstitions and fear.

Here is this son of India.
With tearful eyes, he sits
without wealth and respect and only tears.
Oh ma! Who shall come to his aid
in these dark times!
            Yet how long will he cry!

Seven hundred years float in tears
staying in *Swadesh* under *Videshi* rule
cannot any more bear your anguish.
Within India lie flames of grief.
My heart shatters to think of that sorrow
and to see Indians in pitiable state.
Anguish of our difficult times
is hard to keep contained any more.
            A fire rages within my heart.

[i] In spite of belonging to the progressive Tagore family, Jnanadanandini did not write about her stay in Europe. Much later, her daughter Indira Debi Chowdhurani, in *Puratani*, gives us some information about her mother's stay in England. She records the incidents as she heard from her mother but this work is mostly comprised of personal anecdotes and domestic life with almost no ethnographic details.

[ii] Devendranath has written an interesting account of their early phase of marriage in *Pagoler Kotha* (Tales of an eccentric) where he addresses Krishnabhabini as Kajalani. This account also points at the companionship in their marriage which was not so common in the nineteenth century domestic space.

[iii] This term has been used by Julie F.Codell in an article, 'Reversing the Grand tour: Guest Discourse in Indian Travel Narratives' implying that most of these Indian visitors in London were "both welcomed by Britain's hospitality and imperial British citizens." (174)

[iv] P.C.Mazoomdar's documentation of his voyages to England, America and an Asian country Japan in his book *Sketches of a Tour Round the World* is a case in the point.

[v] Krishnabhabini was going through a major crisis while in England. Her only daughter, Tilottama, was married off at an early age of nine years and they, being in England, could not stop it. But none of her personal crisis is mentioned in the text of *Englandey Bangamahila.* Simonti Sen in her edited volume of *Englandey Bangamahila* includes a few poems composed by Tilottama which give a glimpse into the crisis of the mother-daughter relationship from the daughter's perspective.

[vi] In this discussion I have used W.F. Rae's translation of Hippolyte Taine's *Notes on England* as the columns in the Daily Times, coming out in 1872, could not be accessed. There is another translation of Taine's *Notes* published in 1958 by Edward Hyams but since it is a much later work, I have not taken that into account.

[vii] In nineteenth century Bengal, *babus* were the foppish upper class men known for their lavish and idle life style. They were at the butt of ridicule by the nineteenth century intelligentsia and find a place in many social and literary works of that period.

[viii]In nineteenth century a number of people from Bengal went to healthier climate of the Western parts of India to improve their health. It had almost become a custom with the middle class Bengali population.

[ix] By the phrase 'muslim parsi' the author perhaps is referring to those people who though originally Persian,had later embraced Islam under the Mughal rule.

[x] The author uses the word *'firingi'* here which can mean an Anglo-Indian, Eurasian or a European. I have translated the word as Eurasian or European because the sense in which she uses it is not clear.

[xi] Ramesh Chandra Dutt in his work, *Europe e Tin Batsar*or *Three years in Europe* gives a similar description of these boys in Aden, calling them 'sea-animals' or *jalajantu* (7)

[xii] Ashwin—a month from the Bengali calendar which falls in the months of September–October.

Jesth— a month from the Bengali calendar which falls in the months of May–June.

[xiii]*Sharat* is the Bengali name for a season that comes after the rains and precedes autumn. In the winter countries like England, France, Italy, it is not present, and therefore it does not have a counterpart in English. This shows how geographical difference becomes one of the factors of limits of translatability.

[xiv] A month from the Bengali calendar which falls in the months of October–November.

[xv] Goddess Sashthi is said to be a form of Durga. She is generally accepted and worshipped as the goddess responsible for the well-being of one's sons and daughters.

[xvi] It is the formal rice eating ceremony for a Bengali new-born when the baby is given cereals to eat for the first time.

[xvii]Romesh Chandra Dutt's *'Europe e tin Batsar'*or*Three Years in Europe* has a similar comment. He says, "Napoleon Bonaparte had said that the British are a race of shopkeepers. He could have also said that they are just a race of advertisers" (19) (my trandslation)

[xviii] Bengali month, stretching from mid-December to mid January of English calendar.

[xix] Those men who spent a major part of their time and money in making themselves look good were termed as *fulbabus* of Bengal.

[xx] A Hindu warrior Goddess

[xxi] Describing a typically Hindu custom where a person puts his shawl or some other piece of cloth around his neck before bowing down as a mark of deep respect. .

[xxii] A reference to William M Thackeray's *Book of Snob* and *Vanity Fair*.

[xxiii] After the Queen's Proclamation in 1858, Queen Victoria was not just looked upon as the Empress of India but also as a benevolent mother, responsible for her Indian children's well-being. This sentiment prevailed throughout her reign and was most visible after her death in 1901 when Indian newspapers carried black borders and contained descriptions of numerous condolence meetings organized for her. All kinds of recreational programmes remained cancelled and eminent personalities including Rabindranath Tagore wrote articles in commemoration. For more details see, Paul, Prashanta. *Rabijibani,* Vol IV: 1301-1307. Kolkata, Ananda.

[xxiv] They are officially designated as the Master of Wardrobe and the Mistress of Wardrobe.

[xxv] A Bengali sweet dish usually made of rice powder.

[xxvi] An old form on Indian currency, not in use now. 16 annas make a rupee.

[xxvii] Tagore in *Europe Probashir Patra* devotes a considerable space to the British ladies who spend their time just on fashion and flirting. "They all are either daughters or widows of the upper class men—they have servants and therefore need not work … only one major work is left for her … and that is , of adorning herself." (Tagore 129) (my translation)

Tagore, Rabindranath. *Europe Probashir Patra*. Kolkata, Visva Bharati, Reprint B.S.1393

[xxviii] The word *babu,* as discussed earlier, refers to those nineteenth century men who spent their time and money in luxury and foppery. But interestingly, though it is used for men in Bengali society, Krishnabhabini confers this on the rich and idle English women given to laziness.

[xxix] Though the author presents an almost utopian view of women's education, it was not until 1878 that the University of London opened its doors to women. According to the brief history of the institution provided in their official website "in 1880, four women passed the BA examination and in 1881 two women obtained a BSc."

[xxx] Victorian novel was dominated by women authors, many of whom have obliviated from public memory in the later years. Nineteenth century saw prolific novelists like Mary Elizabeth Braddon (1835-1915), also known as the "queen of circulating libraries" who authored about eighty books; George Eliot (1819-1880), one of the most learned and scholarly writers of her times, whose chief concern was the contemporary society and women; Elizabeth Gaskell (1810-1865),

immensely popular in her times though not remembered much by posterity, her most popular work was *Mary Barton*, her contribution to the 'condition of England' novels along with Dickens, Disreili and others. There were many more women novelists in this period, the Bronte sisters, Jane Austen, Mary Shelley, Fanny Burney to name a few.

[xxxi] The outer part of the house where the master of the house received his visitors. The inner quarter was totally cut off from this part and women were not allowed here.

[xxxii] *Sura* in Sanskrit refers to the drink of Gods and in Bengali means alcohol or spirit. The author by combining *devi,* goddess with it makes an ironic reference to the goddess of alcohol and points at the extreme fondness of the British towards the habit of drinking.

[xxxiii] Most of the Indians travelling to England have focussed upon this evil of English culture. Nineteenth century Bengali society looked upon alcoholism as one of the greatest evils and a sure route to doom. Public drinking being absent from our society, it was something which struck the Indians hard when they came across it in England.

[xxxiv] It is the third month of the Bengali calendar corresponding to mid June to mid July in English calendar.

[xxxv] The eighth month of the Bengali calendar, falling in the period of mid November to mid December.

[xxxvi] The season immediately following the rains in India is called *sharat.*

[xxxvii] *Magh*, the tenth month in Bengali calendar refers to the period between mid December to mid January, which is the coldest time of the year in India.

[xxxviii] Hemchandra Banerjee (1838-1903) was an important Bengali poet inspired by patriotic ideals and a member of the Brahmo Samaj. His

writings also dealt with women's issues and the injustice meted out to women in the nineteenth century.

xxxix Bankim Chandra Chatterjee (1838-1894) was an important Bengali novelist. His most famous novel was *Anandamath*, based on a patriotic theme which also contained the song *VandeMataram*, which was later accepted as the national song of India. He was one of the forerunners of the cultural revivalist movement in Bengal.

xl Fagging was a tradition followed in the English public schools till late twentieth century where the senior boys of the boarding house kept the junior boys as their 'fags' to do them personal services. The system was much like that of domestic helps in their houses and taught the boys various forms of housekeeping. At times it took evil turns and senior boys exploited the younger ones.

xli Pandita Ramabai (1858-1922) was one of the first women reformers in the nineteenth century India. Initiated into education by her liberal father, Ramabai continued her studies on her own after becoming an orphan at the age of 15-16. She and her brother wandered to various places before moving to Calcutta after the death of her parents. There she was bestowed with the title of *saraswati* and *Pandita* because of her learnings. Her marriage to Bipin Beharidas Medhavi, a lawyer, was quite a revolutionary one because she being a Brahmin girl had married an untouchable. This marriage was shortlived as Bipin Beharidas died early. Ramadevi, left with her only daughter Manorama went to Pune where she established the *Arya Mahila Samaj* for the upliftment of women. From there she sailed for England in 1883 to teach Sanskrit in Cheltenham Ladies College. There she embraced Christianity which turned her almost instantly in to a villain, a traitor in the eyes of her contemporary nationalists. In spite of the controversies surrounding her she continued her work for women throughout her life.

xlii Devotional songs associated with the *bhakti* tradition of Hinduism, Sankirtans are performed in public gatherings. The lead singer often accompanies his songs with appropriate physical movements and his followers take the cue from him.

xliii Tappa is a semi-classical Indian vocal music, usually sung by the *baijees* or songstress for a select, often affluent audience, mostly males. The lyrics speak of extreme romantic love.

xliv Panchalis are narrative folk songs of the Bengal region deriving their sources from mythologies, epics or *mangal kavyas.* According to some thinkers these later gave rise to the *jatra* performances. By using *sankirtan, tappa* and *panchali* the author is trying to find some kind of equivalence for her audience in Bengal. But the three are very diverse from each other, in terms of style, audience and place of performance which then raises question regarding her effectiveness in finding equivalence to the songs of 'Salvation Army' for her readers at home.

xlv From 25th December the day starts becoming longer, so it is referred to as *borodin* or long day.

xlvi *Shasthi* marks the beginning of celebration for the Bengalis during the *Durga Puja.*

xlvii The Indian concept of cleanliness was very different from the English concept. In the *Europe Probashir Patra*Tagore well highlights this difference. "There is a big difference between the cleanliness practiced in our country and that here. Here cleanliness is born out of a sense of art and beauty while in our country there seems to be a distinctive consciousness regarding the essence of cleanliness... Here people do not rinse their mouth after eating because spitting water out while rinsing looks very ugly." (Tagore, 86)

xlviii 1 Ser equals to 0.933 kilogram.

xlix This double exclamation has been used by the author in the original text.

Printed in Great Britain
by Amazon

58486171R00162